Critical Guides to French Texts

125 Brassens: Chansons

Critical Guides To French Texts

EDITED BY ROGER LITTLE, WOLFGANG VAN EMDEN, DAVID WILLIAMS

BRASSENS

Chansons

Sara Poole

Lecturer in French,
University of Reading

Grant & Cutler Ltd
2000

ISBN 0 7293 0424 8

DEPÓSITO LEGAL: V. 4.467 - 2000

Printed in Spain by
Artes Gráficas Soler, S.A., Valencia
for
GRANT & CUTLER LTD, 55-57 GREAT MARLBOROUGH STREET,
LONDON W1V 2AY

Contents

For Andy and Viveca

Prefatory Note

Two collections of the texts of Brassens' songs are currently available: a 1991 Editions du Seuil reprint, in the Point Virgule series, of *Poèmes et Chansons* (Editions musicales 57, 1973), and *Les Chansons d'abord*, in the Livre de Poche series, Librairie Générale Française, 1993. Both include various texts never recorded by Brassens himself; the former also reproduces poems by others which he set to music.

My thanks to Mme Eveline Giron, and to Mrs Kate Blinstrub and colleagues, for the time; and to Professor Roger Little as Advisory Editor.

S.P.

'It is the best of all trades, to
make songs, and the second best
to sing them'
Hilaire Belloc. *On Everything*

Introduction

Initially deemed scandalous; provoking polemics both within and beyond artistic circles; denounced in the name of French good taste as vulgar and offensive, then attracting growing public interest and favour; finally praised as a unique (and uniquely French) treasure, jewel in the crown of a national heritage now identified with what it once reviled... France relishes her most cherished monuments getting off to a controversial start. Today the 'vertigineusement ridicule' Eiffel Tower is the most visited attraction in Paris — and the 'flatulences ... d'un faux chanteur, d'un médiocre compositeur, d'un quelconque parolier' (57) are as familiar to at least two generations as *Aux marches du palais* or *Le Temps des cerises*. They are regularly aired on radio programmes, feature in new compilations, are recorded by those younger artists they and their creator inspired (selling very well), appear in their written form in de luxe and paperback editions and have been pressed into service as texts for commentary in public examinations. Eiffel's *dame de fer* has come to symbolise the French flair for daring, stylish innovation. And Georges Brassens has come to symbolise — the French.

   Precisely why this should be so is by no means obvious in that, unlike the Impressionists, certain *cinéastes*, fine wines, Yves Saint-Laurent, etc., Brassens is singularly unsuited to the export market, Francophiles excepted. Whereas the Eiffel Tower from its conception attracted both French and foreign visitors, eager to buy the myriad souvenirs of their visit Parisian businesses were equally eager to provide, the work of Brassens was and is a particularly French pleasure. Thus the notion of his incarnating Frenchness, personifying *à la* Marianne an intangible French quintessence, is not one imposed from the outside by foreign observers, but is instead a home-grown appreciation, surfacing for the first time in the late 1950s. By 1966 journalist Danièle Heymann would observe that Brassens' songs depicted 'la France telle qu'elle fut, telle que toujours elle s'espère: frondeuse, généreuse, amoureuse, vigoureuse'

(*72*, p.39), and Jean Monteaux affirm that 'à travers son œuvre, chacun trouve son compte. Et c'est la somme de ces individualités qui représente l'universalité française du personnage' (*74*, p.14). The judgement was no sooner formulated than it appeared a worn truism. When Brassens died, scores of other commentators sought how best to render an identical sentiment, singer Claude Nougaro proving both the most concise and the most elegant in observing that 'son chant coïncidait avec le génie de son peuple' (*1*, p.12). Almost a decade later, musician Eric Zimmerman was to describe him to all intents and purposes, and with a decidedly Jungian flavour, as a French archetype: 'Brassens fait partie de la conscience collective et de l'âme du Français moyen' (*21*, p.90). And in an article commemorating the week that would have seen Brassens' 70th birthday but in fact marked the tenth anniversary of his death, *Libération*'s Christian Leblé would conclude: 'Ça ne s'appelle pas une vedette, c'est un miroir' (*81*).

The image is telling, and highlights a fundamental question raised by Brassens' work: what image, exactly, is reflected back at the French by a body of writings the consensus holds to be as no other impregnated with their own character? And how is it to be interpreted? If his rise to fame is comparatively easily explained, what of his continuing popularity — what of the Brassens myth? Is the fervent individualist understated revolutionary or mere *rouspéteur*? Are those for whom Brassens was and is primarily *poète-anar[chiste]* closer to or further from the mark than those persuaded of his 'essential conservatism' (*50*, p.281)?

That such contrasting views about the self-same artist and his work can be held, and justified, is less surprising than might at first appear if one examines certain of those ambiguities displayed by both. Thus for example charges of sexism and chauvinism levelled at one whose artistic universe contains so many varied and tenderly evoked, defended or praised women, are as defensible as claims for his feminism, in part because of the equivocality inherent in the frequent use of the first-person narrator in songs in such differing veins as, say, *Saturne* and *Le Mauvais Sujet repenti*. (The climate of the greater part of critical writing devoted to Brassens being uniformly warm and its tone almost invariably appreciative and affectionate, however, such 'charges' or 'claims' are never of the table-thumping variety, and indeed many commentators, faced with such issues, seem to take refuge in the kind of *réponse de Normand* that would have delighted their subject. Paul Ghézi can thus draw to a close his study on the representation of woman in the Brassens canon by pointing out that 'elle n'attire pas toujours la sympathie et nous serions alors tentés d'évoquer une certaine misogynie de l'auteur si toutefois le narrateur et Brassens se confondaient' (*11*, p.148) — a matter, naturally, that each of us is to consider him/herself free to resolve as (s)he pleases ... conditionals *à l'appui*.)

Similarly vexed is the issue of the *non-engagement* (*vis-à-vis* the colonial wars in Indochina and Algeria, or the demonstrations of May 68) of the anti-militarist rebel whose *Mauvaise réputation* had, in 1952, brought outraged servicemen in the audience at the Les Trois Baudets club swiftly to their feet and into the wings in protest (*52*). Some, including his friend writer Jean-Pierre Chabrol (*77*, p.14), see here merely confirmation of the heightened sense of responsibility Brassens regarded as being the (fair) price exacted by fame from those it favours; he was very sensible of the weight his huge following would place on his every public word or gesture, and determined not to make up others' minds for them (*Le Vieux Normand* would seem to bear this out). But Lucien Rioux, author of prefatory essays in the Seghers two-volume collection of Brassens' songs, seems at a loss to explain what he patently sees as incomprehensible non-participation, observing that 'même l'explosion de mai 1968, durant laquelle ... les jeunes quittent leurs facs et leurs lycées pour aller crier dans la rue leur dégoût des fausses valeurs qu'il a toujours dénoncées, leur mépris des pouvoirs qu'il méprise lui aussi, le laisse sinon indifférent, du moins silencieux' (*5*, p.64). And the two relative clauses drive home the implicit reproach...

Hovering question-marks such as the above, the relative importance of individual freedom, religious hypocrisy, etc., are essentially provoked by Brassens himself in that they directly concern what he said, or did, in person or in his writing; any controversy to which they may give rise is his 'responsibility' in the same sense as are, for example, contrasting readings of the same songs. But the 1967 decision of the Académie Française to award him its prestigious Grand Prix de Poésie was not of his doing in the same way (indeed Brassens had always been exceedingly chary of the application of so loaded an epithet to his songs). The choice was popularly applauded, but provoked outrage in some quarters: reacting to it, Robert Poulet poured scorn on an age apparently seduced by 'de la fausse poésie sur de la mauvaise musique' (*46*, p.95), and Alain Bosquet (who would be awarded, and who accepted, the same honour the following year) famously titled the piece he wrote for *Combat* 'Brassens? Pourquoi pas Fernandel?' (*75*). Yet others sat firmly on a fence of hyphens and talked of *chansonniers-poètes* or *poètes-chanteurs* or *auteurs-interprètes de chansons poétiques*. Rioux, clairvoyantly discussing the matter a year earlier, had the humility — and the sense — neither to prevaricate nor dogmatise about interpretations of the word 'poet': 'J'ignore la définition réelle du mot' (*38*, p.243) he, and he alone, admitted.

The prize-winner himself as a rule steered clear of the term, later explaining to Philippe Nemo that he had started out writing poetry, but that 'au moment où je me suis aperçu que je n'avais pas de génie, je me suis dit que j'allais me consacrer à la chanson' (*1*, p.183). The phrasing would seem to suggest that Brassens regarded poetry as both different from and superior to song. But in fact the comment merely points up (yet) another ambiguity essential to the artist and his work, for Brassens not only confirmed to Jacques Charpentreau that 'bien sûr, la poésie et la chanson c'est la même chose' (*8*, p.60), but also assured Jacques Vassal that 'la chanson est l'art que je place avant tous les autres' (*21*, p.356).

So — in opening an edition of Brassens' texts at *La Mauvaise Réputation*, always the first entry, are we really discovering *homo gallus* (version 20th-century-courtesy-of-the-Middle-Ages), *par excellence*? If so, does this suffice to explain the popularity of the man and the work?

Are ambiguous issues such as the putative misogyny or apparent inaction cited *à titre d'exemple* above indications of actual limitations or rather interpretations that can be qualified/refuted? And what of those Brassens claimed to raise with his 'propagande de contrebande' (*7*, p.197)?

Is René Fallet's 'pléonasme [qu'est] Brassens poète' (*78*, p.30) more or less accurate than, or complementary to, Guy Béart's 'homme-chansons' (*14*, p.112)? Was the controversy over the Grand Prix de Poésie any more than a *Tempête dans un bénitier* 'médiatique', and what can we learn from it of Brassens' standing, then or now?

Such questions tend to arise automatically in a consideration of this unique body of songs. The present study hopes to address them, in the course of an examination of both thematic and stylistic aspects of texts which, often for more than forty years, have (sometimes within the space of one and the same verse) contrived to shock, amuse and move their ... listeners.

There — *listeners.* 'Le grand mot', as Fallet wrote of *Hécatombe*'s 'anarchie', 'est lâché. La couleur annoncée.' Brassens no more wrote for the printed page than did Shakespeare and it would be a travesty to reduce to marks on paper what is primarily intended to be heard. The question of whether or not these texts may or may not constitute poems is one that will be returned to, but they are in any case not *just* texts (or not *just* poems); they are part of what is designed as an indivisible whole — a song — complete with melody and accompaniment. And while technical discussions of matters musical will not be entered into, the effect of a specific rhythm or melody may sometimes of necessity be evoked. Because for Brassens, if not for Brid'oison, *tout commence par des chansons*.

1. Beginnings

If in the mid-1930s Charles Trenet had materialised out of a cloudless sky, tossed *la chanson française* a cap and bells and pinned a fetching blue flower to its breast, the '50s saw Brassens shamble over to it, jab his pipe in its ribs and say 'Boo!', not entirely aggressively, but firmly. (Before offering it his arm and escorting it on a long, leisurely stroll.)

The time was the spring of 1952. The euphoria of the Liberation had long since abated but the war had left the youth (specifically) of France a certain moral-emotional legacy with which many of Brassens' songs would not fail to strike a chord. Anti-militarism, for example, was looked on more favourably at this time, and until roughly the fall of Dien Bien Phû (1954), than at any time since (France, one recalls, having been more or less continuously at war since 1939). The global war which had maimed and killed so many Frenchmen had been entered into by a different generation whose values were now suspect, and from which it was important to establish and preserve a distance. For the young, there was a world to be rebuilt, and it was going to be different. This was therefore, as Louis Barjon has stressed, and despite the popularity at the time of the PCF (Parti Communiste Français), 'une génération avide de liberté, hostile aux embrigadements, aux slogans imposés, aux disciplines totalitaires' (*44*, p.57). Freedom was no abstract concept to these young people and the liberty of the individual was understandably a prized notion — although one requiring a recognition of realities that were not always the most palatable.

Thus fantasy and frivolity, so inspiredly and necessarily provided by Trenet and others during the bleak years of the Occupation, were no longer the order of the day. Man's capacity for inhumanity to his fellow-men had been revealed in all its fathomless horror and there was no reason to suppose it had been eradicated with this particular bout of blood-letting. The younger generation, which had also seen the score-settling and witch-hunts of the immediate post-war period, had little reason to trust the values of those carrying them out. Doubt concerning fundamental issues such as direction and identity surfaced in contemporary thought and literature, a reaction against that conviction of God's being on one's side which had helped precipitate a conflict the world was still reeling from. Such convictions had gone hand in hand with certain fixed ideas on what was and wasn't done (morally, sexually, politically), said or believed. Whereas if the rising generation could be sure of anything it was that nothing was as intrinsically oxymoronic as the *idée fixe*.

Finally there was also at the time a sense of the importance of getting back to certain (French) basics; there was in the air what Jacques Vassal has termed 'un besoin de retour aux vraies racines de la culture française (et non plus d'un "retour à la terre", de vichyiste mémoire), un désir de renouer avec une tradition poétique et chantée, qui remonte à l'époque des troubadours' (*21*, p.95). This climate translated into an appreciation of authenticity. The 'amour toujours' song tailor-made for glamorous stars lit from behind and backed by complete orchestras now seemed shallow, over the top; the self-accompanying singer-songwriter was ushering in a new age.

This is not to say that the foregoing briefly sketched outlook was shared by all. It characterised above all the younger Parisian generation — and, in general, the kind of spectator who frequented Patachou's Montmartre cabaret, knowing that anti-conformism was *de rigueur* (and that he might find his tie scissored off if the hostess felt his appreciation lacked warmth). But their elders — and those who could afford more established venues such as the Villa d'Este on the Champs-Elysées — would be less enthusiastic about attacks on an army still sensitive to the defeat of 1940, or an undermining of figures of authority at a time when the dignity of France was being carefully rebolstered. The values they had been brought up with constituted the one touchstone they could still find sense in. And the hits of the '20s and '30s had used little informal language (unless for comic effect) and made no mention of loss of virginity, attacks on the police, testicles, one-night stands, sex manuals, etc. Anything that did was bound to smack strongly of heresy...

March 1952, then, and Brassens, at almost thirty, and after years of disappointment, had finally had his talent recognised by people who knew what to do with it. Having initially sought merely to have his songs included in the repertoire of established professional singers, he had been persuaded to sing some of them himself, despite an aversion to performance and no experience. His first paying public chez Patachou would hear six songs, the recordings of at least three of which were instantly banned from the airwaves (*7*, p.329). Having waited this long for an audience Brassens was not going to break his public in gently. The first song he offered: *Le Gorille*.

If from the mid-sixties the 'fox-trot en boogie' (*35*, p.245) of *Les Copains d'abord* announced his imminent entrance on stage, this role was until that time played by *Le Gorille*, whose shadow/ silhouette looming on covers of early records and sheet music also constituted the primary visual referent associated with Brassens. Written whilst its author was revelling in Rabelais (*18*, p.44), the song had the attraction of rather shocking novelty — and it also incorporated some of the characteristics that would come to be known (*faute d'adjectif*) as 'typical of Brassens'.

Thus the initial verse's periphrasis ('... un endroit précis / Que, rigoureusement, ma mère / M'a défendu d'nommer ici'), the first of many such witty circumlocutions, instantly establishes what is common to almost all those songs featuring an unspecified 'je': the narrator, it conveys, is a *friend* of the listener, on rib-elbowing terms. This sense of complicity is reinforced in verses two, four and five where the audience is addressed directly, and the seal is put on it by the companionable first-person plural of the final verse: 'Ça nous aurait fait rire un peu'. It is significant because for Brassens' public, given no reason to think otherwise, the singer was inextricably bound up in the 'je' of those songs generally deemed to be conveying a personal point of view. The Brassens persona would become an entity in its own right to the extent that Brassens himself occasionally referred to himself in the third person, or again differentiated between 'Brassens' and 'Georges'.

As important for the initial impression as that speedily established complicity is the originality of the comic subject matter of what is after all a song 'with a story', complete with four 'speaking' characters apart from the narrator. (Brassens is very deft in introducing direct speech in his songs, which in turn ensures that few relative clauses or attributative complements need dilute what has by definition to remain a very concentrated piece.) The tale pauses in the seventh verse to recap on the situation, thus creating momentary suspense. The eighth sees the unimaginative figure of authority not only abducted, but being treated by the gorilla as that other stereotypical figure of authority, the school-master, treats recalcitrant pupils ('Il saisit le juge à l'oreille'), thus adding to the humiliation. And the ninth similarly stresses the infantile nature of one invested with such responsibility ('Maman!'), as contrasted with his pomposity in verse six.

Various other factors also contribute to the song's instant appeal. From the point of view of the narrative, the old woman's unexpected attitude to the escape of the gorilla amuses. For the ear there is the attraction of the distinctive, alliterative refrain, and some of the more novel rhymes ('obligé de'/'des deux'; 'guenon'/'que non'). Linguistic richness is used to comic effect in the manipulation of register (the uncomplimentary, familiar 'femelles' of verse 1 contrasting with the zoological specificity of 'quadrumane' in verse 5). Overall it should also be noted that this is a very visual song, from the (censored) close up of the opening lines, the travelling shot of the next few verses and the fade out of the end.

If much in this song, then, was of instant and enjoyable access, it is less certain that the stance against capital punishment implicit in the last verse — in those final lines André Sallée aptly qualifies as 'stupéfiants de densité' (*17*, p.26) — would have been immediately seized upon. Certainly the bald facts of the subject matter of the previous eight verses would suffice to account for *Le Gorille*'s being banned from the airwaves until Europe 1 started up in 1955. And it is by no means obvious that when one Madame Galibourg, 'femme du bâtonnier de l'ordre des avocats de Saint-Nazaire, a personnellement cassé sa bague en applaudissant "Gare au gorille"'[sic] (*56*) it was in fervent agreement with those sentiments almost covertly expressed in those last lines. After all, as on the linguistic level his penchant for periphrasis indicates, Brassens prefers a tangential approach which occasionally takes time to percolate through: 'Je n'ai pas dit: "Mort à la peine de mort", bien sûr, parce que ce n'est pas mon style', he would later explain somewhat less indirectly (*1*, p.188). It is thus of interest to note that the song could and does appeal on different

levels, appreciated either way as an attack on a traditional figure of
authority.

Whilst *Le Gorille* would provoke gasps, laughs, and cause a
public even despite itself to mouth the alliterative eight-syllable
refrain, it was not necessarily what most attracted all those who
stayed to listen to the sweating, scowling colossus whose extreme
discomfort was almost palpable. Patachou herself, to whom Brassens
would always remain indebted, and who seems unerringly to
recognise talent in performers and potential in songs, has since
observed that when first she heard *La Mauvaise Réputation*, 'cette
chanson m'a fait l'effet d'une gifle. J'étais sonnée' (*16*, p.163).
André Vers has written of the 'jubilation' he felt on hearing for the
first time the song that would come to stand as a kind of Brassens
statement of faith (*88*, p.165). Perhaps an odd reaction, for beneath
the wit and cynicism a sinister undercurrent paves the way for the
bleakest of conclusions. There is a relentless and threatening
progression; the narrator's neighbours begin by merely speaking ill
of him, go on physically to mark him out, and then rush at him *en
masse*. The final verse's prophecy that they will hang him is
significantly in the future, and not the expected conditional, tense;
society, it suggests, does not hesitate when it comes to eradicating
those perceived as dangerous because different.

It is of course the unabashed individualism that attracts in this
finely honed piece. The initial couplet, by openly bragging of the bad
opinion in which the narrator is held ('sans prétention'), sets the
tone. Although the third line ('Qu'je m'démène ou qu'je reste coi')
seems to suggest that he cannot win, it becomes obvious that he has
partially provoked a hostile reaction both by staying in bed on 14th
July (was this what so outraged those servicemen who sought
Brassens out in the wings?) and flooring an angry peasant in pursuit
of an apple scrumper. His point (reiterated four times) is of course
that, while his behaviour may go against the norm, his right to it
should be defended provided it does no harm; he himself sees that
others often want to behave differently, but, crucially, has made that
distinction he would wish they might make with respect to him and
can stand back having noted that 'Cela ne me regarde pas'.

The robust individualism points up the excesses of that herd
instinct Brassens was to despise all his life, and doubtless struck

chords in those who had only comparatively recently discovered some of the atrocities for which it had been responsible during and after the war. Those, for example, who zealously organised the head shaving of women suspected of consorting with the enemy probably saw themselves as 'decent folk', and were probably seen as such by others (cf. *La Tondue*). (A few years later Ionesco would stage his chilling account of the deadly 'rhinoceritis', his translation into memorable physical form of the epidemic spread of fanaticism and mass hypnosis pushed to the extreme.) The text of *La Mauvaise Réputation* is, as Pierre Caratini has noted, 'très violent, très sombre' (*21*, p.193). And bizarrely, as André Comay indicates, 'la mention des infirmes contribue à donner au texte son agressivité' (*9*, p.37). But its somewhat surreal humour elicits a smile, as does the odd innovative or particularly successful rhyme ('que'/'qu'eux', 'quatorze juillet'/'mon lit douillet'). One of the forms of wordplay Brassens particularly favours is the (sometimes spooneristic) rejuggling of idiomatic phrases and clichés, and the transformation of the set image 'petit bonhomme de chemin' into 'chemin de petit bonhomme' is both ingenious and adds to the overall tone of injured innocence the verse seeks to convey. And despite the mention of the biblical prophet of doom, all is not lost — the villagers may be unable to find a satisfactory rope...

It seems certain that one of the other four songs wrung out of the wretchedly ill-at-ease performer was *Hécatombe*, comic *tour de force* reaffirming that talent for innovative rhyme, periphrasis ('je les adore / Sous la forme de macchabé's'), the juggling of idioms ('à propos de bottes' translates as 'without rhyme or reason', the onions being an original addition) and introducing the celebrated neologism 'gendarmicide'. Another was *Le Mauvais Sujet repenti*, in which the first person narrator assumes the role of procurer offering technical advice to an inept prostitute, certain risqué rhymes ('confesse'/ 'jouer des fesses', 'popotin'/'sacristain') peppering this counsel. That he has his own moral code, his 'pride', is established in the song's punchline, wherein it becomes plain that 'flics', as distinguished from the belittled 'gendarmes' of *Hécatombe*, frequent, and thus greatly depreciate in the pimp's estimation, his erstwhile *protégée*, leading him to deplore what he sees as her lowering of standards and to conclude sorrowfully that 'Y'a plus d' moralité

publiqu' / Dans notre France...' The disdain expressed for the forces
of order is in the penultimate verse extended, as so often in Brassens'
work, to those regarding themselves as upright, irreproachable
citizens; the young girl catches a venereal disease and infects her
protector, who discontinues the relationship, observing 'Comme je
n'étais qu'un salaud, / J'me fis honnête ...' The sanctimonious,
sinister horde of 'braves gens' last seen hunting a rope to hang the
owner of the 'mauvaise réputation' resurfaces here, acting as
elsewhere in the Brassens canon as red rag to a bull.

A bull; a gorilla, naturally; a bear both because of his size and
the 'mal léché' impression his stage-fright unfortunately gave ... the
music critics who swiftly found their way to chez Patachou or a few
weeks later to Jacques Canetti's Les Trois Baudets were severally
and collectively inspired to produce almost uniformly excited copy
featuring a veritable bestiary of comparisons. The trend never lost
favour; Claude Sarraute alone, over little more than a decade,
converted her 'grosse bête' into a 'gros oiseau prisonnier' which then
metamorphosed into 'un éléphant' only to be recast as a 'grizzli' (*58;
59; 62; 64*). Some eschewed more exotic fauna in favour of redneck
rusticity and wrote of an 'apprenti bûcheron' (*54*) or, later, a 'paysan
endimanché' (*60; 61*). The earliest review would seem to have
appeared in *France Soir* (also the first place in which he is referred
to as 'le troubadour de Sète', and as, simply, 'ce poète'). However
they couched it, one thing the reviewers almost without exception
stressed: Georges Brassens was a name to watch.

Thenceforth, while not every review was favourable, nor every
song appreciated, nor every audience enthusiastic, Brassens became
ever more widely known (five singles released in 1952, three in
1953, four in 1954 together with three LPs), heading the bill at the
Bobino variety theatre a year after his stage debut and winning the
Grand Prix de l'Académie Charles Cros (comparable to the Booker
prize in literature) for his first album barely twelve months later. By
any standard his rise is impressive; so too is the way in which his
appeal extended itself, his image metamorphosed. Less than a decade
after Patachou presented to the public what it pleased so many to see
as a *fauve*, and specifically an apparently grouchy bear, *Combat*'s
critic, not one whit tongue in cheek, was applauding the latest from

'notre Nounours national'. One sign of an evolution it is of interest to explore more closely.

For it had been an unexceptional student, albeit one with a 'feel' for poetry, ear for song, and a prodigious memory for things deemed of interest, who left Sète in the midst of the Phoney War under a cloud that at the time appeared to his family almost blacker than those shortly to engulf the nation. His association with what it pleased the local press to refer to as 'mauvais garnements' had just resulted in his receiving a 15-day suspended sentence for robbery (cf. *Les Quatre Bacheliers*). Brassens' parents decided against his continuing at school; he would instead, to his gratification, go to Paris, where his maternal aunt ran a boarding house (and owned a piano).

Three months' work at the Renault plant ended as France capitulated; for the next two years, working for the occupying forces being an option neither he nor his aunt considered, Brassens taught himself to play the piano and gave himself, thanks for the most part to the library of that XIVth arrondissement he was learning by heart, an intensive course in the poetry and literature of each period or movement that took his fancy. And he wrote — a few hundred poems, most later discarded, others returned to, a few (eleven and thirteen) grouped into two slender volumes, the second of which, *A la Venvole*, was privately published.

This was a single-minded and a strange existence for a young man of twenty who had already concluded that 'les normaux sont trop nombreux' (7, p.39). The same fervour for poetry, and the self-discipline that got him up at five to exercise, read and write would set Brassens apart the following year when the STO (Service du Travail Obligatoire) sent him to Basdorf, and a BMW factory manufacturing aeroplane-engines. A year to the day after his departure (8th March 1943) for the work-camp, he returned to Paris on leave (and with at least a dozen songs in his luggage); rather than go back to Germany, or cause problems for his aunt, he accepted the offer of an erstwhile liaison and loyal friend Jeanne le Bonniec (Jeanne Planche since her marriage in 1942) and her husband to hide out in their tiny and basic home in the impasse Florimont. And while six years (again to the day) later Patachou would push him firmly into the spotlight, this was not an eventuality the unskilled, unemployed and penniless 23-year-old could possibly have predicted.

Thus the early part of 1944 saw Brassens essentially cut off from society to an almost unimaginable extent, a fact he would underline in a documentary interview with Jean-Paul Chabrol: 'J'étais vraiment en marge de la vie. [...] J'étais quand même une espèce d'épave, une épave studieuse mais une épave. [...] Je m'étais déjà créé un univers dans lequel n'avaient cours que les idées, les pensées, et les sentiments que j'acceptais. Je vivais très peu dans le présent et dans le milieu ambiant' (*14*, p.22). The reading — in fact the true study — and discovery of a plethora of poets was intensified. Unable to venture out in daylight, Brassens exercised in the minuscule courtyard; deprived of the piano, he composed with the aid of an old banjo, beating out rhythms on Jeanne's old wardrobe. Recognition of a growing talent neither seemed, nor was, just around the corner.

2. Major Themes (one)

With the Liberation, little would change (although Brassens could at least once again make use of the library of the XIVe). What Pierre Berruer has termed 'un sentiment anarchiste, un rejet de ces institutions imbéciles qui [... avaient] conduit les hommes à se dresser les uns contre les autres' (*4*, p.49) representing his attitude towards the society he was watching from the sidelines, it was indeed unlikely that a disillusioned dropout *avant la lettre* should be swept up in the unfurling wave of patriotic sentiment and its wake — rough-justice reprisals. The armistice brought the return home of those with whom Brassens had worked in Basdorf. With some of them, and with friends from Sète, he founded the 'Parti Préhistorique' to promote values other than what he perceived as the prevailing moralising and materialism, and tried to launch *Le Cri des gueux*, the title an echo of Jean Richepin's 'La Chanson des gueux', extracts from which he would set to music. When this project failed to get off the ground for lack of funding he turned to writing for the French Anarchist Federation's *Le Libertaire*.

While he would only contribute articles to this weekly for a few months these pieces are of great interest because they constitute the earliest published indications of Brassens' preferred themes and favourite targets. Thus the police take centre stage in several, each of which cites incidents (a detonator mistaken for a wireless valve; a cyclist jolted by a police whistle into knocking over and killing the police officer wielding it; shots fired at an escaping suspect instead felling a sergeant) chosen to underline the premiss that 'dans la profession de Pandore, point n'est besoin d'avoir à sa disposition un intellect perfectionné'. Politicians, journalists, profiteers, the rich in general and 'les gens de bien' or 'les honnêtes gens' are taken to task. The military and their 'crétinisme hyperbolique' are not spared. Perhaps more interestingly advocates of communism and in particular of its Soviet strain provide material for several articles, one reproving a *L'Humanité* journalist for whipping up hatred of the

Nuremberg judges, others, including a musing text on autumn, essentially deploring the notion of politically correct poetry: 'Eluard, Aragon et consorts demanderont au bon papa Staline l'autorisation de chanter la chute des feuilles ...' The Church, finally, is a bitterly derided target, Catholics being called upon to impute to 'leur fétiche tout puissant, Jésus-Christ, la conception et la réalisation des sanguinaires mises en scène que sont les guerres mondiales', Christ also being accused of general complicity in 'la corruption, la vénalité et la pourriture des individus et des temps' (*23*, pp.86–106). All in all, as an apprenticeship for one who was to continue a national tradition of anti-establishment *chanson*, the months served at *Le Libertaire* could not have been bettered.

Indeed through all these youthful pieces runs in addition a common thread that is the passionate defence of the individual, translated into a rejection of all those power-groupings (police, clergy, military, the commercial world) representative of authority within a society deemed corrupt. And there is also a relentless indicting of anyone (including two named journalists and Maurice Schumann, who had for four years broadcast anti-Nazi propaganda on the BBC) presuming to tell others what to think and do, particularly should such exhortations advocate sentiments of hatred or vengeance, when indeed they were not encouraging the ultimate sacrifice in the name of some suspect absolute (in this case 'la patrie'). These texts exemplify perfectly an anarchism Brassens defined as 'une sorte d'attachement viscéral à la liberté et une rage profonde quand des hommes veulent imposer quelque chose à d'autres hommes' (*23*, p.24). They can also be seen as fertile humus in which patently germinated a goodly number of Brassens' most successful works. The following (and by no means exhaustive) investigations aim to illustrate the translation into song of several of the above preoccupations.

The forces of law and order

Brassens' policemen (*flics, argousins, gendarmes, cognes, pandores*) fall somewhere between the Keystone Cops and Mr Plod. They are 'par natur' si ballots' (*Brave Margot*) and at the very least

(*Hécatombe*) under-endowed. Bystanders rejoice in seeing them injured (or worse: the luckless 'flic' of *La File indienne* is fatally stabbed 'à la joie du public'). Rival factions unite to attack them: 'Dès qu'il s'agit d' rosser les cognes / Tout l' monde se réconcili''. Contact with them contaminates, as noted above of the indignant 'Mauvais sujet repenti', and as is apparent from the detail that Corne d'Aurochs' cousin holds a senior position in the force. While the lover of married women in 'A l'ombre des maris' began with policemen's wives, he reveals this shamefacedly: 'Cette faute de goût je ne la commets plus'. And the elderly man obsessed with seeing the navel of a policemen's wife dies at the precise moment his wish is about to be realised...

The farcical flatfoot is, however, redeemed in two similarly structured songs where with (somewhat dubious) humour several stereotypes are reversed. Thus *Don Juan* presents a valorous vicar, a merciful 'militaire', a broad-minded 'bonne sœur' and a 'flic qui barrait le passage aux autos / Pour laisser traverser les chats de Léautaud'. And *L'Epave*, conversely, shows a pauper, a student, a worker's wife and a prostitute stripping and then reporting a drunk, to whose rescue comes a concerned policeman, whose first thought is to offer his cape to the nonplussed narrator: 'Moi, dont le cri de guerr' fut toujours ''Mort aux Vaches!'' / Plus une seule fois je n'ai pu le brailler'. Both songs are illustrative of Brassens' ability not only to stand on their heads certain *idées reçues*, but similarly to upturn theories one might have held with regard to 'anti-stereotypes' as featuring in his own canon.

All of the above are humorous in tone. Only *L'Orphelin* cites 'un animal / De flic qui me voulait du mal'. The most sinister of references — because unadorned — to the police is to be found when thanks are expressed to the discomfited stranger, watching 'lorsque les gendarmes m'ont pris', of the *Chanson pour l'Auvergnat*.

The root of all evil

Brassens' attitude towards money — something he survived a long time having next to none of — and its effects on those obsessively concerned with it is, particularly in the early songs, one of puritanical suspicion. Thus the idealistic tone of the editorial he and André Larue wrote in 1946 for the ill-fated *Cri des gueux* stands in sharp contrast to the exuberant vituperation of the pieces for *Le Libertaire*: the piece claims to be representing 'une poignée de camarades qui s'insurge contre l'Argent, non contre l'argent dispensateur de nécessités ou des plaisirs, mais contre le pouvoir ignoble et injuste qu'il confère' (*13*, p.134).

It is in songs such as his *Les Croquants* — a word Brassens redefines as meaning rather 'prosperous landowner' than revolting seventeenth-century peasant — that Brassens points up the limitations of wealth by having a young girl prefer to the uncomprehending 'culs cousus d'or' suitors whose attentions — and not whose means — she enjoys. Once again standing the conventional outlook neatly on its head he shows his 'croquants' making do with those generally considered 'les filles de bonnes mœurs', here presented in essence as those who have held out for the highest bid. Where their suitors are merely unimaginative and dissatisfied (and rich), these young women are portrayed as calculating materialists; the two parties, it is suggested, (richly) deserve each other. In similar vein, *Comme une sœur*'s 'espèce de mercanti', 'un vrai maroufle, un gros sac d'or' may temporarily benefit from the hapless hero's unsuccessful suit, but he is likely to die soon, leaving the latter the task of consoling his widow.

Le Père Noël et la petite fille is the more sinister for its understatement. The repetition of the second line of the refrain 'Il a mis les mains sur tes hanches' has a cumulative effect of menace, and the conclusion, wherein we learn that the relinquished past may have been both hard and harsh, but that it was also 'le joli temps des coudé's franches', is concentrated, just as is *Le Gorille*'s final message, into two almost throwaway lines. Essentially this Father Christmas is merely a more exclusive version of those 'vaches de bourgeois' exploiting the inappropriately named 'filles de joie' of the *Complainte*. It would seem particularly perverse to see in this enumeration of monied gestures anything that is not disdain for those who seek to buy others and compassion for those forced into selling their only asset. Michel Barlow and Paul Ghézi, however, both appear to find the piece ambiguous, hedging their bets in almost identical terms[1]; Charpentreau classes the young girl as a 'sainte-Nitouche' (*8*, p.83); and Lucien Rioux unaccountably sees the sugar-daddy figure as genuinely kind.

In the lyrical *Chanson pour l'Auvergnat*, his first song to find favour with the general public *en masse*, and arguably his best known (*4*, p.101), Brassens is merciless towards the 'croquants', principal villains in a celebration of selfless humanity striking chords in every listener. Refusing the needy stranger fire (warmth, hospitality, a life-force), finding amusement in denying him food, and laughing to see him led away by the police, they show him a lack of charity which transforms the humble offerings of the song's heroes — wood, some bread, a rueful smile of solidarity — into gifts worthy of the Magi. These 'croquants', we feel, are first cousins to those indirectly evoked landowners responsible for the poverty of 'pauvre Martin' and his like, condemned to a lifetime of working 'le champs des autres / Toujours bêchant ...' They are also by the same token related to the 'vieux nabab' of *Le Myosotis*, the 'vieux barbon' of *Les Ricochets*, *Jeanne Martin*'s 'béotien' of a grocer and to the 'Philistins' and the 'Oiseaux de Passage' of the two poems by Richepin Brassens chose to set to music.

In keeping with the violent tone of some of the *Le Libertaire* pieces, the relatively early *Celui qui a mal tourné* (c. 1957) in fact invites us to sympathise with the murder of an anonymous passer-by 'en or massif' (thus prefiguring *L'Assassinat*). But it is in this exceptional. As a rule, Brassens claimed to prefer to out-and-out denunciation, or condemnation, approaching his target at a tangent, as it were. Thus in *Auprès de mon arbre* the final verse does not state in so many words that the narrator is rich but miserable — merely that he used to inhabit a shabby attic room and have a regular turnover of female visitors, whereas now:

---

[1] Barlow (*2*, p.27): 'On ne sait donc si l'on doit se réjouir [...] de voir l'amant-papa-gâteau déverser des hottes de cadeaux sur la belle: va-t-il vraiment lui offrir "le joli temps des coudées franches...?"'; Ghézi (*11*, p.62): 'On ne sait pas dans ce cas là [*sic*] si l'on doit vraiment se réjouir de voir cet amant "papa gâteau" déverser sa hotte de présents sur la belle. Va-t-il vraiment lui offrir un bonheur durable?'

J'habit' plus d' mansarde,
Il peut désormais
Tomber des hall'bardes,
Je m'en bats l'œil mais,
Mais si quelqu'un monte aux cieux
moins que moi, j'y pai' des prunes

Jingoists, 'flaggery' and armchair generals

The military and those glorifying war and its trappings are a
favoured target of one persuaded that 'military intelligence' is an
oxymoron it can be fatal not to appreciate as such. On occasion
Brassens contents himself with sideswipes — thus *La Mauvaise
Réputation*'s protagonist remains in bed (but at what cost?) during
the military parades of the 14th July; the 'mauvaise herbe' vaunts
tongue in cheek 'le déshonneur / De n'pas êtr' mort au champ
d'honneur', the hero placing flowers on a war memorial in *La Rose,
la bouteille et la poignée de main* is characterised as 'gâteux', and in
Les Sabots d'Hélène it is to the three 'capitaines' of folklore that is
imputed an inability to see beyond appearances of which the song's
narrator makes the most. Frequently, however, and with lesser or
greater degrees of irony, war, patrioteering and related issues take
centre stage in what were some of his most controversial pieces.
While precise dating of the composition of many songs is a
hazardous enterprise and an examination of copyright dates not
necessarily more enlightening, it would seem safe to say that the
decade 1962-72 saw the production of the most contentious (if not
belligerent).

This period thus launched what an anonymous critic in *Le
Canard enchaîné* referred to as 'cette étonnante ballade [...] qui est, à
mon avis, la plus fine et la plus percutante des chansons
antiguerrières' (*65*). *La Guerre de 14-18* cites a variety of historical
conflicts, from the Trojan to the Second World War, purporting to
find an admirable or praiseworthy aspect to each. Its narrator,
ostensibly an ex-serviceman ('Mon colon'), has the indecency to
attempt to rank them using the vocabulary of school merit systems,
according, it must be supposed, to their bloodiness. Thus he can
generously opine of WWII that 'Elle fut longue et massacrante / Et je

ne crache pas dessus', and that in general 'chacune a quelque chos'
pour plaire'. While hoping the god of war will come up with 'un vrai
délice', he indicates in an identical couplet ending verses 1 to 5 that
WWI (in which France lost more men than in any other conflict) is
his particular favourite. The song lambasts all those whose nostalgia,
usually for the companionship of a period they had the good fortune
to survive, contributes to romanticising or justifying war. The tense
change of the final verse — in essence the punch-line — can be
interpreted as stressing the stupidity of this 'ancien combattant',
World War One of all wars being seen as the one in which young
men were called up specifically to die, and thus being the one he
would have been least likely to survive. (Alternatively André Sallée
sees it as revealing that the narrator has been stringing along a
gullible military commander: 'Autrement dit: mon colon, vous avez
le bonjour!', *17*, p.130.)

The mid-sixties saw the release of the two Brassens songs
giving rise to the most virulent polemics: *Les Deux Oncles* and *La
Tondue*. (It is of course a measure of just how sensitive the French
were to certain *prises de position* arising from WWII that the
reaction to these songs should be so violent almost a generation
later.) Criticism was not by any means confined to commentators on
the Right: *L'Humanité*, for example, wondered if Brassens realised
'qu'il a commis une mauvaise action et deux mauvaises chansons',
and voiced its disapproval in two articles lamenting that what it
interpreted as 'cette glorification de l'attentisme, cette assimilation
des bourreaux et de leurs victimes' should be the work of someone
the paper generally much admired: 'La lutte "contre les extrêmes", la
"sagesse" de celui "qui-ne-fait-pas-de-politique", on connaît la
musique. Chansons que tout cela — mais chansons de Brassens?'
(*68; 69*).

It is easier to understand why the former carefully crafted text,
recounting in impeccable alexandrines the opposing loyalties and
deplored deaths of one uncle supporting the Allies, and another
supporting the Axis, should have hit nerves. There are essentially
two aspects of *Les Deux Oncles* most likely to have caused offence.
The first, concentrated into verses 5, 6 and 7, claims that the uncles
and presumably their like (i.e. all those who plumped for one side or
the other, i.e. nearly everyone) are no longer of any interest ('Tout le

monde s'en fiche/fout). The second is the reiterated notion that 'il est
fou de perdre la vi' pour les idé' — that 'aucune idé' sur terre est
digne d'un trépas' — which is the element *L'Humanité* appears to
have found the most offensive.

It seems clear that what Brassens intended to have predominate
was the theme, hinted at in verse 13, that what is essentially immoral
is causing someone else — because that is a power one wields as a
military chief — to die for ideas that you decide to impose upon
them: 'les seuls généraux qu'on doit suivre aux talons, / Ce sont les
généraux des p'tits soldats de plomb'. Certainly this is what he was
at pains to stress to Danièle Heymann: 'Moi, je ne délivre pas de
messages. Je ne rebâtis pas le monde. [...] *Les Tontons* [...] c'est une
chanson d'amour et de tolérance qui dit aux gens : "Méfiez-vous, ne
vous laissez pas mener."' (*72*, p.41).[2] But trusting to the tale rather
than to the teller would seem to demonstrate that not enough weight
is given to this apparently main theme. And as for 'pas de messages'
(as if 'Méfiez-vous', etc. was not a message in itself), it is worth
noting that there are other (usually subsequent) instances, for
example the long 1979 interview with Philippe Nemo, where
Brassens defends and indeed vaunts his propagandising: 'Je suis un
des premiers à m'être engagé dans les chansons. Et d'une façon très
nette' (*1*, p.188).

La Tondue saw Brassens in 1964 treating events Eluard had
felt compelled to portray as they happened twenty years earlier in his
'Comprenne qui voudra'. But where Eluard's 'victime' (of the head-
shaving imposed by kangaroo courts on women suspected of
consorting with Germans) is just that: a target, an unhappy,
bewildered 'enfant perdue', Brassens' is but barely sketched in, and
indeed disappears half-way through the song so that the narrator's
cowardice and eloquent synonyms for 'cheveux' can take centre
stage. The song closes on, as it were, a close-up of the kiss-curl he
has felt moved to pick up; its rightful owner, and the suffering she

---

[2] A June 1947 piece, 'La Chanson', for *Le Libertaire,* cites in the warmest of
tones an extract from a Raymond Asso song:
> Et tous les morts de faim et de froid,
> Ceux qui sont morts pour toi, pour moi
> Pour la patrie et pour la loi.
> La loi de qui! La loi de quoi. (*23*, p.116)

has undergone in the losing of it, have faded into the background. Brassens may have condemned so barbaric a custom elsewhere with great conviction; this vehemence would however seem lacking in a piece whose focus, as the most cursory of analyses indicates, is early on shifted from the hapless 'tondue' to the bystander-narrator.

Eight years on Brassens returned to that theme he had avowedly intended to be central to *Les Deux Oncles* and released the much more homogeneous *Mourir pour des idées*, this time avoiding direct reference to any specific conflict and concentrating instead on those ('les saint Jean bouche d'or', 'les boutefeux' — references to religion and warfare) who incite others to self-sacrifice. A quarter of a century after Sartre's *Les Mains sales* the song stresses the transient nature of ideas and ideologies for which individuals may at a given moment be prepared to die (or to kill), and points out that each variation on wholesale slaughter has to date not brought about a noticeably improved world ('l'âge d'or sans cesse est remis aux calendes').[3] Again offence was taken. Claude Réva's *D'accord, vivre pour des idées* also enlisted the alexandrine in an eloquent reproach:

Ils n'ont pas demandé ceux qui sont morts pour elles
D'être passés ainsi de la vie au trépas
Ils ne l'ont pas voulu, la mort n'est jamais belle
C'est un peu grâce à eux que nous sommes encore là.

                                                        (*82*, p.24)

Maxime Le Forestier, who has always included works by Brassens in his repertoire and who in 1996 recorded an entire album of twelve of his 'petits bonheurs posthumes', is categorical: 'Ma génération, celle de Mai 68, a très mal pris cette chanson: à vingt ans, mourir pour des idées, c'est quelque chose d'évident', but recognises that courage was required to issue it in such volatile times (*17*, p.181). Certainly those who had expected some kind of

---

[3] One is put in mind of some of the work of W. D. Ehrhart, American poet and Vietnam veteran, an example being the following extract from his 1984 collection *The Outer Banks and Other Poems* (Adastra Press, Easthampton, MA; p.23): 'If I were young again, / I could do it all / differently: / [...] — anything / but kill / somebody else's enemies / for somebody else's reasons'.

statement from Brassens (at the time grappling with one of his recurrent kidney stones) during May 1968 were again disappointed, unable to reconcile a known and admired anti-authoritarian stance with what they saw as an abnegation of all principles they held dear.

Brassens was frequently called upon to field questions on his lack of *engagement* in the protest movements of May 1968. He always answered on similar lines: 'Même si je n'avais pas été malade, qu'aurais-je pu faire? Aller sur les barricades et dire aux gens: voilà ce qu'il faut faire, voilà ce qu'il ne faut pas faire? Et de quel droit? A quel titre?' (*17*, p.181). (It would seem important here to recall his initial intense antipathy to the spotlight and lifelong aversion to the star-system.) *Le Vieux Normand*, a song originally intended for what was his last album, but in fact never recorded by Brassens himself, and which could well date from 1972/73, deftly sums up his position. It takes its inspiration from the adage that has it that a 'réponse de Normand' is ambiguous or non-committal — and a 'réponse de vieux Normand' presumably more so — and in its last verse stresses that the truth, being an idea like any other, can be a question of fashion and belief. This is why the narrator returns repeatedly to the advocating of individual choice (and individual responsibility): 'Crosse en l'air ou bien fleur au fusil, / C'est à toi d'en décider, choisis!'

That final 1976 album included *Les Patriotes*, wherein the irony of *La Guerre de 14-18* and the selected invalids of *La Mauvaise Réputation* are brought together to deplore the glorification of war by (save in the last verse) its survivors. Unrecorded by Brassens however are the early *La Guerre*, which stresses how that glory fades as one approaches the field of battle: 'Qu'on nous dise : "Faut y aller!", / On est dans nos petits souliers'; *Quand les cons sont braves*, with its bellicose general: 'Dès qu'il s'en mêle, on compt' les morts'; *Tant qu'il y aura les Pyrénées*, with its endearingly honest refrain

> S'engager par le mot, trois couplets, un refrain,
> Par le biais du micro,
> Ça s'fait sur une jambe et ça n'engage à rien,
> Et peut rapporter gros;

and *La Légion d'honneur*, dealing humorously with the behaviour incumbent upon those awarded it. Finally, *Honte à qui peut chanter*, one of the very few songs Brassens wrote to mention living (or recently dead) people, and recent events, shows him on the defensive, exasperated at having to point out that 'pas le seul', 'comme tout le monde', 'ainsi que tout un tas', etc., he lived as normally as possible during each of the conflicts in which France had been involved during his lifetime — and that not doing so, not singing along to the latest Chevalier, Montand or Brel release, would not have affected the outcome one jot.

It would thus seem fair to say both that some of the most *engagées* of Brassens' songs are those attacking war and the military mentality, and that this theme is a regularly evoked constant. Exactly how close such matters were to his heart is not in question, but it is of interest to note a comment made by André Halimi (convinced as of the fifties that 'on chantera Brassens dans mille ans'): 'Que l'on soit de droite ou de gauche, le thème de l'antimilitarisme paie toujours' (*34*, pp.16, 19). Or, as Brassens' biographers Marc Robine and Thierry Séchan have it: 'L'antimilitarisme, c'était sa vie, mais c'était aussi son fonds de commerce' (*16*, p.249).

Seul(ette) suis et seul(ette) veux être

The notion of art created specifically for the purposes of organised politics was, as is clear from his attacks on Aragon and Eluard in *Le Libertaire*, anathema to Brassens. It is thus not surprising that his own work should so emphatically proclaim both the rights and indeed the superior moral integrity of the individual insistent on carving out his own path. The belligerence of those youthful articles can be seen to fuel certain early songs such as *La Mauvaise Réputation* (discussed above) and the relentlessly nose-thumbing *La Mauvaise Herbe*, whose first-person narrator survives a war he did not believe in, frequents a prostitute who will not charge him, and refuses to follow a road others see as having no alternative :

> Les hommes sont faits, nous dit-on,
> Pour vivre en band', comm' les moutons.
> Moi, j'vis seul, et c'est pas demain
> Que je suivrai leur droit chemin.

Assuming an injured tone he then enquires of those who resent his thriving 'en liberté' 'Pourquoi, Bon Dieu, / Ça vous dérange / Que j'vive un peu ...'

Such open antagonism however would soon give way, in the 'chansons anarchisantes' (*22*, p.59), to one of two distinct moods: that of wry abdication in the face of human absurdity, or a darker, fatalistic severing of all contact with it. The latter attitude is rarely more than obliquely hinted at. It is disguised in a conceit such as the *Discours de fleurs* (a song never recorded by Brassens):

> Car je préfère, ma foi,
> En voyant ce que parfois,
> Ceux des hommes peuvent faire
> Les discours de primevères.
> Des bourdes des inepties,
> Les fleurs en disent aussi,
> Mais jamais personne en meurt

and evoked humorously and at length in *La Rose, la bouteille et la poignée de main*. But despite the uncharacteristic 'on' (i.e., essentially, if not grammatically, a first-person *plural*) of the narration, it colours the whole of the sober *La Visite*, described by Vassal as '[une] très grande chanson sur le racisme' (*82*, p.52), and most obviously inspires the arresting choice of adjectives in lines 14 and 15 of *La Marche nuptiale*, where 'l'œil protubérant' economically conjures up the crowd of gawping onlookers, and 'futile' carries the full weight of an outsider's scorn.

A less trenchant, bemused distancing from his fellows counterbalances that sombre tone. It inspires two memorable first-person alexandrines which biographers of Brassens delight in and unhesitatingly proclaim autobiographical: 'Je vivais à l'écart de la place publique / Serein, contemplatif, ténébreux, bucolique' (*Les Trompettes de la renommé*). The 'grand chêne' patently shares this distaste for the public eye as is summed up in another alexandrine ('Il vivait en dehors des chemins forestiers') meaning much the same thing. And *Quand les cons sont braves* shows us a world of '"braves" cons', with whom the narrator aligns himself, and self-important 'crétins sectaires' contriving to make the earth 'une pétaudière'.

The exception to the two extremes of attitude posited above bristles with the intransigeance characteristic of the most uncompromising of its predecessors. *Le Pluriel*, released in 1966, not only multiplies references to striking out alone (its narrator is 'celui qui passe à côté des fanfares', 'qui reste à l'écart', and whose motto is 'bande à part sacrebleu!') but is forcefully and repeatedly scathing about those not inclined so to do. The provocative refrain, maintaining that 'sitôt qu'on / Est plus de quatre on est une bande de cons', together with the enumeration of collective nouns, patently inflamed the Communist Party's lyrical Jean Ferrat, whose album of later the same year would thus feature *En groupe, en ligue, en procession*. The song, as one would expect, proclaims his diametrical opposition — 'Je suis de ceux qui manifestent' — to the stance advocated in *Le Pluriel* and offers a thoughtful caveat : 'on peut être seul et con / Et [que] dans ce cas on le reste'.

In common with all those songs cited above (with the exception of *Le Grand Chêne*) and many others through which may be said to run that 'petit air frondeur', *Le Pluriel* is written in the first-person. This fact, allied to a knowledge of the value Brassens placed on the rights of the individual, encourages a reading of these songs as embodying a genuine profession of faith. And this in turn can elicit and possibly justify reactions such as those voiced by Linda Hantrais (*12*, p.154): 'il est ironique que lui, qui dépend du public pour son revenu, semble mépriser la masse' or Fabrice Venturini (*22*, p.50) who, discussing the arrangements of *Tempête dans un bénitier* and *Le Roi des cons,* suggests that one might be 'surpris par l'avènement de [ces] chœurs [...] quand en parallèle la chanson intitulée *Le Pluriel* met en relief la loi du nombre comme échelle de mesure de l'intelligence humaine'. A literal approach indeed. Essentially, however, *Le Pluriel* would seem to be a logical extension, for one so fervently individualistic, of the intended central theme of *Les Deux Oncles* and *Mourir pour des idées*: one should guard against being swept up to defend idea(l)s imposed upon one from whichever quarter, be it hierarchically, or merely numerically, superior. This is indeed what Brassens is at some pains to explain in the Sève interviews: 'Ce que je refuse, c'est qu'un groupe ou une secte m'embrigade et qu'on me dise qu'on pense mieux quand mille personnes hurlent la même chose [...] Je ne combats pas le pluriel d'entr'aide, ce serait du pur égoïsme. Mon individualisme d'anarchiste c'est un combat pour garder ma pensée libre: je ne veux pas recevoir d'un groupe ma loi. Ma loi, je me la fais moi-même' (*18*, pp.138-39).

In respect of the cloth

Where Brassens' policemen are typically stupid, cuckolded or both, what Michel Barlow has termed his 'policiers du ciel' (*2*, p.37) and their close relatives are generally petty or uncomprehending. Thus *Grand-père*'s *curé* turns away the corpse and its penniless offspring because he holds to the belief that 'Les morts de basse condition, / C'est pas de ma bénédiction'. The priest in *Le Grand Chêne*, referred to as a 'petit saint besogneux' and then as 'le bougre', has the effrontery to express doubts as to whether or not the smoke generated when the unfortunate oak is burnt actually reaches heaven. And the 'putains de moines' of *Tempête dans un bénitier* fail utterly to see that holding mass in mere French deprives that service of the mystery Latin bestowed upon it. Completely incapable of understanding, empathising or much else, finally, is the abbé of *La Rose, la bouteille et la poignée de main*, whom we find 'sortant de la messe ivre mort'.

More strikingly, from choirboy to seminarist, verger to priest, the vast majority of those of the Brassens cast linked even tenuously to the Church are above all lascivious. Wholeheartedly embracing traditional anticlerical views on 'l'hypocrisie sexuelle des dévots' (*2*, p.36), Brassens peoples many humorous, and some provocative, songs with bawdy bishops and lubricious lay-people, some having bit-parts, others playing leading roles. Thus when the news spreads that Margot is breast-feeding her kitten, the choirboys desert the church 'au milieu / Du saint sacrifice' (and of the onlookers they join, the verger is specifically identified); the later controversial *La Religieuse* pictures them masturbating joylessly, their fantasies about and expectations of the titular nun come to nought. When the 'Mauvais sujet' is instructing the inexperienced prostitute in methods of attracting clients it is taken as a matter of course that sacristans will number among her customers. (It is also suggested in the same song that becoming a call-girl is more difficult than following a religious calling, and indeed the daring rhymes which Sallée stresses 'papillonnent autour du sacrilège' (*17*, p.54) drive home that comparison, as 'confesse' is made to echo 'des fesses', and 'sacristain', 'popotin'.) In *Fernande*, one of four characters reflecting on the effects on their libidos of various women is a seminarist; in *Mélanie*, a less well-known but equally bawdy piece, the pious maid with the passion for beeswax naturally works for the *curé*.

Actual clergymen and -women behave identically to, if not worse than, their lay helpers. *Le Moyenâgeux* wistfully evokes the 'nonnettes' and 'nonnains' who 'Ne disaient pas toujours "nenni", / Qui faisaient le mur du couvent' and who 'Comptaient les baisers, s'il vous plaît, / Avec des grains de chapelet'. Similarly sentimentalised is Huguette du Hamel, who turned Port-Royal into a brothel (*12*, p.189 n. 5). *Les Trompettes de la renommée* portrays le Père Duval, the singing priest, as 'surpris aux genoux d'ma maîtresse'. *Misogynie à part* shows its narrator reminiscing about 'la p'tite enfant d'Mari' que m'a soufflé' l'évêque'. And the two Hugo poems Brassens chose to set to music centre around 'le pâtre de ce canton' (*Gastibelza*), 'pâtre' being translatable either as 'shepherd' or as 'pastor', and a nun (*La Légende de la nonne*), both in love in vain.

Two songs redeem clerics. The priest of *La Messe au pendu* sprinkles holy water on daisies, feeds birds with communion wafers but, above all, says a mass for a man whom his parishioners have hanged by way of rough justice. Where Brassens refused himself the opportunity to decry the death penalty in so many words (although ensuring that his signing of a petition to this effect gained maximum publicity), he allows this gallic Don Camillo a resounding 'Mort à toute peine de mort!', thus raising him to the rank of the Auvergnat or the wives of Bonhomme and Hector. Finally in *Don Juan*, hymn to those volleying back received ideas, a 'bonne sœur' charitably warms up the frozen penis of a one-armed man and a compassionate priest saves an enemy antagonist during the Saint Bartholomew massacre.

God

On one level God functions as a conversational tic in many Brassens songs. D. H. Lawrence, resuscitator in *The Plumed Serpent* of a morally repulsive pantheistic religion, superstitiously sprinkled his correspondence with myriad 'D(eo) V(olente)'s; Brassens' exclamations share a similar tone of appeasement : 'Que Dieu te ménage' (*La Chasse aux papillons*), 'veuille le grand manitou' (*Le Pornographe*), 'le Bon Dieu me le pardonne' (*Je suis un voyou*), 'Plaise à Dieu' (*Mélanie*), etc. The god evoked in such expressions is usually the indulgent, paternalistic or avuncular figure encountered in *Le Testament* ('le Dieu qui partout me suit / Me dira, la main sur l'épaule / "Va-t'en voir là-haut si j'y suis"'), *Le Vieux Léon* ('Et si l'Bon Dieu / Aim' tant soit peu / L'accordéon ...'), and in a Paul Fort poem Brassens chose to set to music, *Si le Bon Dieu l'avait voulu*. Capricious, sometimes heavy-handed, unpredictable, He on occasion works to ensure His ways remain mysterious: 's'il existe, il exagère', famously expostulates the narrator of Jeanneton's unlucky chain of events. This is a theme stressed in the lament *Jean rentre au village*, where six of the twelve stanzas unfold bad and worse news and end with the bald 'Le bon Dieu n'est pas gentil'. But He remains, if not approachable, at least familiar, the ultimate irascible patron served by dolts (including *Mélanie*'s saint, 'cet imbécile', who allows a sailor to drown because his votive candle is removed), hypocrites and lechers.

That 's'il existe, il exagère', however, highlights an issue fundamental to both man and artist. Brassens was the son of a fervent Catholic who ensured her son was baptised, attended a religious kindergarten for two years, and took communion — and of the unbeliever whose gentle understated humanism he would openly celebrate in *Les Quatre Bacheliers*, *Ce n'est pas tout d'être mon père*, and arguably *Le Modeste*. His own atheism — or perhaps, more accurately, agnosticism — while as a rule steady, would nevertheless be tried, tested, and never taken for granted. This question of religious faith and the lack of it is returned to again and again in interviews (and not only those conducted by Father Sève) and dealt with in different ways at different times: with a kind of defiance ('Pourquoi Dieu existerait-il forcément. Pourquoi, me diriez-vous, n'existerait-il pas non plus? [...] Eh bien, s'il existe ... c'est un drôle d'oiseau, voyant ce qui se passe'); with irony ('La plupart des gens croient que Dieu existe parce qu'on le leur a dit. Si on ne leur avait pas dit, ils ne l'auraient jamais trouvé tout seuls'); with wistfulness ('J'ai ce malheur de ne pas croire en Dieu') (*16*, pp.262, 260, 256).

Those same or similar qualities naturally inform the songs which deal obliquely or directly with the same issue. In places, defiance translates into irreverence, blasphemy, and a need to shock. *La Religieuse* apparently discomfited Father Sève 'au point qu'il envisagea de cesser toute relation avec le poète' (*16*, p.260), and one is tempted to suggest that it was less the subject matter (of the potentially coquettish nun) that offended, than the cavalier way in which God is hailed ('Bravo, Seigneur, c'est du joli travail!' approves the protagonist, admiring her figure), and the nun's devotion to His son evoked ('On ne verra jamais la corne au front du Christ'). A comparable tone is found in *Le Grand Pan* which pictures a disgruntled Christ clambering down from the crucifix decidedly disappointed in mankind and saying so: 'Merde! Je ne jou' plus pour tous ces pauvres types!' *L'Antéchrist* represents Christ's sacrifice in a particularly unorthodox way, and comments dryly upon it:

> Entre son père et lui, c'était l'accord tacite:
> Tu montes sur la croix et je te ressuscite!
> On meurt de confiance avec un tel papa.

And *Tempête dans un bénitier* is distinguished by a use of the vulgar — 'les fidèl's s'en foutent'; 'putains / De moines' — and by an enjambement arguably 'le plus pervers de toute l'histoire de la chanson française' (*16*, p.261): 'Sainte Marie mèr' de / Dieu'.

Elsewhere the vexed question of belief surfaces directly in witty and ironic pieces which nevertheless have an aftertaste of rancour. *La Ballade des gens qui sont nés quelque part* points up the ludicrous aspects of the kind of regionalism that functions as a microcosm for nationalism and its darker side, racism. It goes on to wonder why God should have permitted the survival and indeed flourishing of these chauvinists and then posits a possible solution to the query: the continuing existence of such individuals, God is informed, is 'preuve, peut-être bien, de votre inexistence'. And here is the crux of the Brassens ethos; he is in his songs, like Orwell's Bozo (*90*, p.149), essentially 'the sort of atheist who does not so much disbelieve in God as personally dislike him'. Brassens' 'God', as noted above, surrounds himself with idiots and deceivers. It is 'les chrétiens du pays' who seem most likely to find fault with the comprehensive father of *Les Quatre Bacheliers* — and who thereby reveal their lack of Christian charity. In *Le Mécréant*, wherein Brassens claimed to present his own views, the narrator may initially protest his envy of blind faith, but is almost immediately attacked (for singing *Le Gorille* and *Putain de toi*) by the kind of believer he has just professed the wish to join. The song ends in a verbal shrugging of the shoulders and again, doubt: 'Si l'Eternel existe, en fin de compte, il voit / Qu' je m'conduis guèr' plus mal que si j'avais la foi'.

Le Sceptique reveals an apparently regretful unbeliever compiling a lengthy list (including Heaven, Hell, God and the Devil) of things he cannot believe in, but concluding 'j'envie les pauvres d'esprit pouvant y croire'. Belief, it is clear, is desirable because comforting — but nowhere does Brassens seem able to evoke a God worthy of belief. Indeed, the little-known *Les Illusions perdues* (or *On creva ma première bulle de savon*) plainly finds God wanting: 'Le bon Dieu déconnait. J'ai décroché Jésus / De sa croix: n'avait plus rien à faire dessus'; and the *Elégie à un rat de cave* wishes the deceased 'des lendemains qui dansent / Où y a pas de Bon Dieu'. The only compassionate God is that of the *Chanson pour l'Auvergnat*, and Brassens makes it clear that He is a construct 'belonging' solely to the good Samaritans of the song. Calvet is perhaps right to discourage speculation by stating flatly that 'toutes ses déclarations sur Dieu et la religion sont celle d'un athée' (*7*, p.250). Believing, in short, is, for Brassens, to be hoped for essentially for its capacity to reassure: *Le Mécréant*'s 'charbonnier' may be 'con' but he is also happy. Religion as opiate; God as Prozac. Brassens never lost his mistrust of the side-effects.

3. Major Themes (two)

Mortality

If *Le Libertaire* provides rich pickings for those seeking the genesis of certain preoccupations of his songs, Brassens' contributions to it by no means prefigure them all. And while the present study does not aim at an exhaustive thematic analysis (Michel Barlow's *Brassens* lists thirty-three entries in an *Index des thèmes* that the most cursory glance reveals as selective) it cannot justifiably omit what are amongst the most prevalent of obsessions typically associated with the work and the man.

Death ('Dame la Mort', 'la Parque') is not entirely absent from those early articles, but appears almost exclusively in connection with incidents ridding the world of some hapless 'argousin immonde'. Death does, however, loom large in the Brassens canon, a fact underlined by all its commentators, but made more of by some than by others (this phenomenon tending on occasion to reveal more about the investigator than the investigated). Angèle Guller, for example, is categorical that 'c'est dans ses chansons sur la mort et dans celles-là seulement que Brassens nous révèle en même temps son amour de la vie ou plus exactement des vivants' (*33*, p.85). But where does Brassens celebrate life and vitality more joyously than in *La Chasse aux papillons*, *Il suffit de passer le pont*, *Les Copains d'abord*, *La Première Fille* — to name but a few? Calvet acknowledges the undeniable presence of death in the songs but asserts that 'les chansons de Brassens ne nous apprennent [donc] rien sur ses rapports à la mort'. Turning from the work to the life and apparently finding excessively morbid his habit of keeping a (labelled) snippet of hair from a mourned pet, or jotting down the date of a dear one's death on an object near to hand, Calvet goes on to describe Brassens' true relations with death as 'cette obsession', 'une névrose obsessionnelle' (*7*, pp.247, 249). After which his concession that 'une psychanalyse se fait difficilement en l'absence du principal intéressé' might be deemed superfluous, details about his own experience of domestic animals and pre Post-it note-taking seeming potentially of more relevance. For Beaufils, however, death is more straightforwardly 'un thème éminemment poétique' significantly corresponding 'plus à la reprise d'un thème littéraire qu'à une obsession' (*3*, p.60). And Rioux (*15*, p.61), an anonymous *Canard enchaîné* critic (*63*) and Hantrais contribute a sense of perspective when they stress 'la plaisanterie morbide' and 'l'humour macabre' characterising certain of those songs in which death takes centre stage, or more simply opine that 'la mort est plutôt un objet d'humour' (*12*, p.115). It is indeed undeniable that schoolboy, gallows or merely black, Brassens' sense of humour often takes the sting out of death, its trappings, its ceremonial.

It is also however of interest to consider Pol Vandromme's observation that 'sa poésie de la vie était une poétique de la vie *cérémonielle*. Sa poésie de la mort aussi' (*20*, p.110; my italics). For while death — its forms, guises, nature — indisputably colours at least a quarter of all the (c. 230) extant songs, there are similarly present in this work the births and marriages preceding it, and also ceremonial occasions of a less official nature, such as those celebrated in *La Première Fille* and *La Non-demande en mariage*.[4] In fact rites of passage of one sort or another abound in Brassens' work, and are rarely conventional in form or in effect. Thus for example he makes of *La Non-demande en mariage* a lyrical love-poem to the 'éternelle fiancée', bemoans in *Le 22 septembre* an end to mourning, but refuses to attach any moral significance to the losing of virginity, opining in *Chansonnette à celle qui reste pucelle*:

> Y'a pas plus de honte
> A se refuser,
> Ni plus de mérite
> D'ailleurs, ma petite,
> Qu'à se faire baiser.

---

[4] Indeed, questioned on this issue by Philippe Nemo ('Vous avez un sens aigu de la cérémonie?'), Brassens, whilst patently reluctant to admit so strong an attraction, is obliged to concur: 'C'est d'autant plus curieux que j'ai horreur de ça' (*1*, p.190).

An 'affective virginity' is a state of grace bestowed upon those, however sexually active, who fall deeply in love; if the adolescent recipient of *Chansonnette à celle qui reste pucelle* is assured that 'on peut / Etre passée par / Onze mille verges, / et demeurer vierge' it is because 'Les fill's quand ça dit "Je t'aime", / C'est comme un second baptême' (*Embrasse-les tous*) — although hardly one ordained by any recognised spiritual body. In short, while the frequency of references to death or to dying cannot be challenged, it is important to place this characteristic within context and note a general fascination with all forms of human celebration and ceremony (why else would an agnostic interest himself in the 'mystère magique' of the Latin mass?).

Looked at thus, one aspect of Brassens' interest in the trappings of death reveals itself as, essentially, an enjoyment of the ceremonial associated with funerals. Over a dozen burials are mentioned in passing, homed in on or anticipated — and remarkably few of these are couched in negative terms. Thus of Corne d'Aurochs, vilified throughout the song dedicated to him for various failings including an incapacity for original thought, we learn that, for the self-same reason, 'L'Etat lui fit des funérailles nationales'. A similar ironical cast is given *Le Temps passé*, wherein death is shown to confer on the most wretched of ages, love-affairs and individuals a nobility entirely lacking in their lifetime.

In *La File indienne* a handful of unlikely characters, including the murderer, joins the funeral procession for the unfortunate 'flic' 'tortillant de la croupe et redoublant le pas'. In *Au bois de mon cœur* the deadpan narrative voice tells of repeated weddings, but also of repeated funerals, both his own, which his friends conscientiously attend. *Grand-père* stages a farce around the assembly, piecemeal, of the bare necessities in burial terms, together with some nimble footwork on the part of both narrator and songwriter, who between them ensure that each of the three individuals approached in vain for help 'a un' fess' qui dit merde à l'autre'. Both *La Ballade des cimetières* and *Les Funérailles d'antan* treat the place as well as the panoply of burial with joyous irreverence. The latter not only offers the particularly remarkable and untranslatable image of earlier modes in matters mortuary when 'les gens avaient à cœur de mourir plus haut que leur cul', but incorporates repetition to great effect in its refrain, ensuring that 'les belles pom, pom, pom, pom, pom, pompes funèbres' sound anything but funereal. *L'Enterrement de Paul Fort*, a text that was never set to music, qualifies the titular event as 'le plus beau jour de ma vie'. And the seamless, haunting 'chef d'œuvre d'intimisme' (73) that is the *Supplique pour être enterré à la plage de Sète*, and which contrives to place each of its listeners squarely in front of his own destiny, leaves us with an impression of sunshine, scented breezes, music, and with that most graceful of *chutes* exhorting us to envy the luck of one 'qui passe sa mort en vacances'.

In general, then, what René Fallet christened 'le cimetière Brassens' is the scene of many a merry funeral. Two notable exceptions, however, cast a shadow hinted at by the 'pauvre fossoyeur' unable to reconcile himself to his task or its inevitability ('J'ai beau m' dir' que rien n'est éternel, / J'peux pas trouver ça tout naturel'). *Pauvre Martin* has the limpidity of a haiku and the simplicity of a late Matisse, and Martin himself is less Brassens' 'soldat inconnu' (9, p.21) or his Pilgrim than his Everyman. His life is bleak and his death a gradual rubbing threadbare, but he bears both courageously, singing as he literally works himself into the ground. Digging his own tomb is, we are made to feel, just an extension of that labouring; what makes this act memorable is the speed and discretion with which it is carried out, and particularly the fact that it is all done thus 'Pour ne pas déranger les gens'. Were we in any doubt on the matter, the much later *Don Juan* spotlights for praise him whose basic philosophy can be summed up as 'ne pas trop emmerder ses voisins', and *Le Modeste*, he who shuns exhibition but demonstrates an understated sensitivity. These portraits sum up Martin, one of the most memorable of Brassens' heroes, in a nutshell. His lonely death contrives to evoke, simultaneously, pity, despair, admiration, solidarity.

The other ambiguous curtain call is that staged in *Les Quatz'arts*, a surreal nightmare wherein the narrator, spectator at what he presumes to be a mock funeral staged by the Ecole des Arts et Métiers, gradually realises that the mourners in tears, the priest, and indeed the corpse are not students contributing to a prank, but genuine — and that he himself is 'le plus proch' parent du défunt'. Qualified by Fallet as an 'œuvre terrible et de désespoir' (10, p.103),

Les Quatz'arts is seen by most critics as a turning point; as André Tillieu has it: "'Les vrais enterrements viennent de commencer". Et ça c'est son père et sa mère' (*83*, p.90), Brassens' mother having died in 1962, and this song being recorded the year before his father died. Certainly no slapstick farces on the lines of *Grand-père* succeeded this piece. It is a macabre and an uncomfortable song — but yet again, with approval of the students' ability to organise the procession 'comme il faut' reiterated eight times, and each element held up to an expert eye for examination, it underlines Brassens' enthusiasm for the ceremonial of the last rites. A literary, but also a real, passion; Jean-Pierre Chabrol has reported that, whenever he baulked at attending yet another funeral with this most sought-after mourner, Brassens, reproachful, would issue the unanswerable ultimatum: 'Si tu ne viens pas à mon enterrement je n'irai pas au tien!' (*16*, p.337).

Burials constitute of course only one aspect of the theme of death as found in Brassens' work. Accounts of them are understandably absent from those songs — and there are several — treating death as a future event. Songs such as *Chanson pour l'Auvergnat* (the future demise of whose three heroes is the subject of each refrain), *Le Pornographe*, the *Supplique* itself, *L'Ancêtre*, *Le Pêcheur*, conjure up future dying essentially to celebrate present living, putting the accent on earthly pleasures rather than dwelling on the end of them. 'Je me sers de la mort', explained Brassens on more than one occasion, 'pour donner de l'importance à la vie [...], pour vanter la vie' (*71*). The anticipating in tranquillity characteristic of the above-mentioned certainly corroborates this stated aim. So too, however, does the lamenting of precious lives cut short, particularly for avoidable reasons, which is what *La Mauvaise Herbe* and *Le Pluriel* (in part), and *Les Deux Oncles* and *Mourir pour des idées* (in their entirety) are concerned to do.

In the same interviews Brassens refers to death as 'une espèce de clown blanc, un faire-valoir', a comparison worth noting. It offers a tangential approach to the personification of death who, damned to femaleness as a result of the vagaries of French genders, appears in the songs as 'La Parque', 'La Faucheuse' or 'La camarde', and is indeed, in the guise of 'Sa Majesté la Mort', shown to be 'no better than she ought':

> Telle un' femm' de petit' vertu,
> Elle arpentait le trottoir du
> Cimetière,
> Aguichant les homm's en troussant
> Un peu plus haut qu'il n'est décent
> Son suaire ...
> (*Oncle Archibald*)

But it also confers a dignity the familiar aliases lack, the white clown being foil to his red-nosed baggy-panted companion, but also the *auguste*'s superior; the one who is to all appearances in control of the act.

Finally worthy of mention is the opportunity frequent references to death offer to one delighting, as Brassens certainly did, in the rich variety of expressions it inspires — in, if you will, the linguistic ceremonial. Conventional euphemisms abound: 'le vieux Léon' is pictured as 'parti au paradis', the cast of *Chanson pour l'Auvergnat* is 'carried off' by the undertaker, and in *Le Temps passé* those of whom no-one now dares speak ill 'ont cassé leur pipe'. The notion of making 'un trou dans l'eau' occurs in *Les Copains d'abord, Je rejoindrai ma belle, Le Vieux Léon*, 'avaler sa chique' in *L'Ancêtre*. As Hantrais has pertinently observed, 'Brassens emploie fréquemment l'euphémisme, non parce qu'il veut éviter le terme direct pour des raisons de tabou, mais parce qu'il exploite le potentiel des images ainsi créées' (*12*, p.147). The notion of 'une mort naturelle' as oxymoron is thus raised in *Le Fossoyeur* and *Bonhomme*; 'la mort dans l'âme' takes on a new and novel sense as it describes the singular protagonist of *La Ballade des cimetières*, whereas in the same song 'funeste erreur' can be interpreted both figuratively and literally, as can 'une figur' d'enterrement' in *Le Fossoyeur*. And *Le Testament* is an ingenious weaving together of many similar expressions, where the impression given seems at first familiar (half of the original structure or idea being retained) and is then recognised as startlingly original — the notion of 'la tombe buissonnière' and of the chrysanthemum as 'la marguerite des morts' (Loved me, loved me not?) — being particularly memorable examples.

Pas des amis de luxe...

If an agnostic sometime anarchist can be accused of holding anything sacred, Brassens put his faith in friendship. His biographers vie with each other to list instances of a legendary fidelity, an impulsive and unstinting generosity, deep and non-judgemental affection. Interviews reveal a Brassens proud of his friendships old and new and ever sensible of what he himself gained from them. If Jeanne and Marcel Planche stand out, as the exceptional couple who took him in and specifically kept him alive for the lean immediate post-war years, it was two erstwhile schoolfriends become journalists, Roger Thérond and Victor Laville, who engineered the fateful audition with Patachou, and the enterprising STO-camp librarian, Pierre Onteniente, who would become Brassens' factotum and lifelong confidant. To the Sète and Basdorf circle of friends would be added those whose attention had been caught by his talent, of which Jean-Pierre Chabrol (*L'Humanité* journalist turned writer-*conteur*) and novelist René Fallet are best known. Brassens prefaced their books, shared with them his literary enthusiasms, tried out his songs on them. They were privileged members of the 'bande de cons' who formed his alternative family and could with justification be seen as the inspiration behind those songs featuring 'les copains'.

Quantitatively, however, the number of the afore-mentioned songs is rather small. Certainly friends flit briefly across the stages of, for example, *Le Fossoyeur*, where they laugh at a grave-digger so ill-suited to his task, or *La Marche nuptiale*, where they pull the oxen yoked to the wedding cart. In *La Fessée* and *A l'ombre des maris* they contribute to the comic effect: in the former, the blow in question is dealt to the very recently widowed wife of a schoolfriend at the unfortunate man's wake; in the latter, the cuckolded husband on occasion becomes such a firm friend of his wife's lover that a liaison which has cooled is maintained solely in the interests of that unconventional friendship. But such instances can hardly be interpreted as illustrative of an ethos. And it would be a mistake to give consideration here to *L'Epave*'s policeman, the passers-by in *Celui qui a mal tourné*, or the protagonists of *Chanson pour l'Auvergnat*, all of whom may well exhibit fraternal generosity but each of whom, far from being his friend, is an anonymous stranger to the narrator. Disinterested, staunch, understated friendship is the central theme of, essentially, three songs.

The earliest recorded of these is *Au bois de mon cœur*. It alternates repetitive verses of a pastoral flavour — in which are likened to each other flowers as located in various woods and the narrator's friends as located in his heart — with ironic observations on the nature of the said friends' companionly devotion. Close to his heart they may be, but that heart is notorious for harbouring those deemed undesirables by others. Such is their affection that his friends will drink their host's water when they have finished off his wine. The narrator, it is then revealed, makes a habit of marrying, his bosom pals considerately attending each ceremony. A final verse of deadpan surreality has these devoted companions similarly present 'each time' he dies. 'Voici des fruits, des fleurs, des feuilles et des branches / Et puis voici mon cœur ...' proffers Verlaine in *Romances sans paroles*. Brassens offers his heart and a metaphor transforming it into a wood: refuge, sanctuary, temple formed of the oaks and pines often referred to in his songs, but also a mysterious, a secret place (he much admired Kipling's 'The Cat that Walked by Himself' who disappears into the Wet Wild Woods), deep, alive, enduring. The image is strong and revealing of tenderness; this is why the leaven of irony, offsetting the emotion, provides such a pleasing contrast.

Le Vieux Léon, released a year later, is a technical *tour de force* (96 lines of four feet each), in the form of a brisk waltz, which functions simultaneously as portrait and as commemoration of all affectionate, uncomplicated friendships. Where *Le Modeste*'s eponymous hero attends friends' funerals with a heavy heart but a dry eye, mourners of Léon choose rather to laugh 'Pour faire semblant / De n'pas pleurer' — and fifteen years after the death of the old musician, they are still moved when they hear the accordion. Like *La Princesse et le croque-note*'s self-denying 'épave accrochée à sa guitare' or the worthy 'joueur de flûteau', Léon is presented as a simple 'jobbing' musician, modest, admirable, memorable. This is a portrait embroidered upon in the Europe 1 interview cited by Vassal (*21*, p.226): 'C'est l'histoire d'un type qui jouait de l'accordéon dans la rue de Vanves, dans le XIVe, et dont nous autres, nous nous foutions un petit peu, quoi, parce que nous n'aimions pas ... ou nous croyions ne pas aimer l'accordéon. Et puis il est mort; alors là on s'est aperçu qu'on aimait l'accordéon, qu'on l'aimait.' And Brassens sums up: 'C'est une déclaration d'amour, *Le Vieux Léon*. L'amitié solide existe toujours, ça continue d'exister comme par le passé'. This conclusion is what should be retained — particularly given that both Charpentreau (*8*, p.88) and Angèle Guller (*33*, p.89) record Brassens confirming that in fact *there was no 'model' for Léon*, that *'il n'a jamais existé, bien sûr'* (my italics). Léon is, then, a composite, a collage; his existence is not an actual truth but a truth of the imagination. He testifies to Brassens' extraordinary ability to transform qualities into characters who then take on both an archetypal and a familiar aspect. In *Bonhomme* Unconditional Loving Loyalty stubbornly seeks fuel for her companion's last hours. Heroic Uncomplaining Endurance in the form of 'pauvre Martin' digs his own grave when his time comes. Léon is the unrepentantly unexceptional friend — no state funeral for this amateur of wine, women and popular music. Mourning his passing is a way of sending a message to all 'friends of friends' recognising the deep and usually unsung ties of affection binding them — ties Brassens himself cultivated and cherished (something obviously to the forefront of Georges Moustaki's mind when he wrote his tribute: *Les Amis de Georges*).

Friendship is also the subject of one of the most popular songs Brassens ('Sétois la Zizanie' to that closest of companions, René Fallet) wrote. By common consent it was to became his 'signature tune'. *Les Copains d'abord* marries its titular theme to an extended maritime metaphor, gains weight from literary and religious allusion, contrasts the latter with a familiar tone and register, and sets these components to what has been defined as 'rock 'n roll ou à peu près' (*28*, p.108). The nautical linguistic framework — 's'aimer tout's voil's dehors', 'C'est l'amitié qui prenait l' quart, / C'est ell' qui leur montrait le nord', 'viré de bord', etc. — a fertile source of images relating human relationships and situations, is returned to in an interview Brassens and Brel gave to *L'Express* in which they discuss the role of song (*71*, pp.30-32). Brassens stresses the communication with others: 'Au fond on pousse des cris pour que les autres entendent, on appelle au secours, on appelle à l'amitié. Je crois que c'est ce que nous faisons [...]. On est des bateaux en détresse. Nous lançons des S.O.S. Moi, c'est ce que je fais à chaque chanson, j'appelle au secours.' But where the reference here is to vessels adrift, the songs, as *Les Copains d'abord* illustrates, centre firmly around boats' crews, like-minded teams of friends 'pulling together', united in common preoccupations, sharing the same direction. Thus the homage to musician Moustache's wife, *Elégie à un rat de cave*, presents her early death as a disembarkation, and evokes her loyalty in terms belonging to the same semantic grouping: 'Tu n'étais pas du genre qui vire / De bord et tous on le savait, / Du genre à quitter le navire'. And most striking is the ending of a piece Brassens never satisfactorily put to music, *Les Illusions perdues*, wherein a disenchanted narrator, lamenting among other things burst bubbles, failed loves and lost gods, decides to hurl himself into the sea:

> Juste voguait par là le bateau des copains;
> Je me suis accroché bien fort à ce grappin.
>
> Et, par enchantement, tout fut régénéré...

In 1969, Henri Colpi asked Brassens to sing *Heureux qui comme Ulysse*, the theme song (inspired by Du Bellay) that he had written for his film of the same name starring Fernandel. Given its repeated assertion that freedom is particularly appreciated 'Quand un ami fait le bonheur / ... sèche vos pleurs', the song certainly echoes the sentiments expressed in *Au bois de mon cœur* and *Les Copains d'abord* (both, coincidentally, also written for films). But it also has in common with these, and with *Le Vieux Léon*, a decided emphasis on the appreciation of the simple, the natural — in short, on the gift of contentment: 'On vivait bien contents / Mon cheval, ma Provence et moi'. (Brassens' 'Modeste' would value above riches 'un seul cheval camarguais / Bancal, vieux, borgne, fatigué'.) Friendship contributes to that contentment if it is not only disinterested, but also characterised by discretion and even diffidence. And these latter characteristics similarly apply to its portrayal. The 'Modeste' avoids exertion so as not to overawe others with his strength, argues with his victor at *pétanque* so as to conceal his pleasure at the win, suffers in silence rather than declare love or show sorrow. *Les Copains d'abord*, finally, relentlessly eschews any hint of what could be construed as praise in favour of repeated negatives ('ce n'était pas', 'y'avait pas'). We learn progressively that this group of friends is generous, open, unaffected, dedicated, loyal and faithful — but only by means of a listing of what they are not. And this tribute to Brassens' personal 'bande de cons' is the more eloquent for it, friendship being, as René Fallet was well placed to observe, 'une chose si sérieuse, chez Brassens' (*10*, p.77).

L'éternelle fiancée versus les emmerderesses

It is an undeniable fact that women loom large in the Brassens canon (even when 'maigrelette'), 'un personnage féminin' being, as Hantrais has it (*12*, p.108), 'au centre de l'action' in many if not most of the songs. This fact has encouraged an establishing of lists, a dividing-up according to various criteria, etc. Thus for example Paul Ghézi investigates three aspects of the sum of the female personages — their physical appearance, social status, and personalities — and comprises such sub-divisions as 'Nue ou habillée'; 'Grosse ou maigre'; 'La mariée - la mère'; 'Elle rit, elle pleure'. And more succinctly, Marc Wilmet lists, in no particular order, those qualities appearing to him defining characteristics: the Brassens woman can be 'imprévisible', 'insaisissable', 'intéressée', 'cruelle', 'fragile', 'tendre', 'magicienne', 'secourable aux esseulés', 'victime de parents cupides', 'jouet des vieux beaux/guerriers fringants/mâles vantards', 'beaucoup plus vulnérable que vénéneuse' (*23*, pp.48-49).

In themselves such statistical data are, at least, informative and sometimes thought-provoking. Problems arise however when, often unaccountably ignoring that other major character, the song's narrator, critics use them to make assumptions about Brassens' (the individual's) attitude towards (real) women. To cite as does Ghézi Baudelaire's 'La Chevelure', and to invoke Jeanne Duval, the actual (half-caste) woman inspiring it, in order to highlight a putative contrasting preference on Brassens' part for blondes (as supposedly revealed in essentially two songs, *Bécassine* and *La Route aux quatre chansons*), seems to me to presume much on slight evidence. The former piece, reminiscent of *Les Croquants*, is of the *Aux marches du palais*, *Raggle Taggle Gypsies* lineage wherein a girl prefers to other wealthier suitors a lover of much more modest means. It deliberately maintains and prolongs a tradition of virtuous cherry-lipped, golden-haired maidens (as opposed to the specifically brunette young woman of easy virtue of *Les Filles de La Rochelle*) much as had Donovan Leitch's *Colours* some four years previously ('Yellow is the colour of my true love's hair...'). The second is a revisiting of four traditional folk-songs (whose heroines have evolved for the worse) which includes the seventeenth-century *Auprès de ma blonde* (presumably because of the ribald potential of 'il fait bon dormir'). Is it not thus somewhat hasty to conclude on the basis of such 'evidence' that 'Brassens semble avoir un penchant pour les blondes' (*11*, p.9)?

Similarly Fabienne Pascaud, in a deliberately provocative piece 'Misogynie à part, tu parles!' (*84*, p.64), opens with the oft-cited:

> Elle n'avait pas de tête, ell' n'avait pas
> L'esprit beaucoup plus grand qu'un dé à coudre,
> Mais pour l'amour on ne demande pas
> Aux filles d'avoir inventé la poudre...
> (*Une jolie fleur*)

to give credence to her portrait of Brassens as a 'macho bon teint'. But replaced in context this is the lament, tinged with some bitterness, of an abandoned lover whose broken heart is no longer worth offering anyone else; the (spent) fury, in short, of a man scorned. The apparently equally controversial

> Ell' m'a dit d'un ton sévère :
> 'Qu'est-ce que tu fais là?'
> Mais elle m'a laissé faire,
> Les fill's, c'est comm' ça ...
> (*Je suis un voyou*)

is similarly no illustration of personal conviction concerning female inconsistency but part of an account given by a rather endearingly blunt, practically minded 'voyou'. One ignores at one's peril — and at the cost of misrepresenting the texts — the anonymous first person narrators (to which we will return) of so many of Brassens' songs.

Enumeration of the female characters peopling the songs also encourages the generalisation that Brassens only ever describes 'la bonne fille, facile ou non, qui sait la valeur de la gentillesse; et la garce, la "jolie fleur dans une peau de vache", cruelle et sans esprit. Pas de place pour la femme intelligente, ou pour la volontaire, ou pour l'indépendante' (Rioux, *38*, p.240). Rioux himself deflects such an argument by pointing out that the male characters are 'also' 'braves types' or 'salauds', and furthermore that intelligence is not a quality Brassens is interested in underlining in any of his characters of either sex. But in fact there are many, and not only minor, female characters who cannot be thus pigeon-holed: Pénélope; the 'favorite' of *Saturne*; 'ma mie' of *Rien à jeter*; the 'rat de cave' of the '*Elégie*'; the 'maîtresse d'école'; the bride of *La Marche nuptiale* — to name but a few. And several lacking neither in spirit nor in wit, amongst whom can be numbered the Briviste forcing from the 'maréchal des logis' a 'Vive l'anarchi'!' (*Hécatombe*); the handyman's wife lamenting her spouse's fixation with finding spots 'où / L'on peut encor planter un clou' (*Le Bricoleur*); *La Fessée*'s widow, struck on the rump and appealing for reparation ('Aï'! vous m'avez fêlé le postérieur en deux!'); and Cendrillon drily pointing out certain idiosyncrasies in the behaviour of her lustful lepidopterist:

> Je présage
> Qu' c'est pas dans les plis de mon cotillon,
> Ni dans l'échancrure de mon corsage,
> Qu'on va-t-à la chasse aux papillons.

The above caveats aside, there are several aspects of Brassens' treatment of female characters in his songs that are worthy of (non-generalising) note. Perhaps the most obvious of these is his portrayal of woman as, if not exclusively, often predominantly, a sexual being. Thus those pieces characterised by their 'grivoiserie', 'paillardise', 'verdeur' or 'gauloiserie' (and which Maxime Le Forestier has had the frankness to term 'chansons de cul', *82*, p.69) concentrate less on male sexuality (*S'faire enculer*; *Fernande*) than on a variety of 'female drives' (*Les Radis*; *Mélanie*; *La Nymphomane*). This is also true of many of the 'merely' risqué or the humorous songs (*Les Casseuses*, *La Religieuse*, *Le Cocu*, *A l'ombre des maris*, *La*

Traîtresse, etc.). And while a few anonymous narrators (those of *A l'ombre des maris, L'Orage, La Traîtresse*), and characters such as Bonhomme or Lèche-cocu, are overtly or implicitly unfaithful to their own spouses or active in cuckolding others, 'épouses volages' and their spinster equivalents litter the work, unrepentant, unrepudiated.

    Less Rabelaisian but equally worthy of note are those songs praising disinterested promiscuity, and which by their very nature credit both sexes with identical and equal appetites. *Les Croquants* is an ode to the 'chair' fraîch'' and 'grand cœur' of a girl who has never compromised her instincts, her own code of honour ('N'a jamais accordé ses faveurs / A contre-sous, à contrecœur') and whose desires lead her to 'faire peau neuve avec chaque saison' and with the nearest like-minded lad. The wistful nostalgia of *Les Amours d'antan*, with its folk-song Suzettes, Margots, nymphs and shepherdesses and its Greek and Roman gods, essentially laments a pre-war, pre-Aids and (at least in part) mythical (pre-pill) straightforwardness in sexual commerce where each partner is on exactly the same footing: '"Je te plais, tu me plais ..." et c'était dans la manche'. And particularly relevant here is the exquisitely tender *Embrasse-les tous* which wholeheartedly encourages an exhaustive trying-out of potential life-partners and manages simultaneously to become 'un hymne à la pureté' (*10*, p.90) whose romantic message is clear: Love is what matters; follow your heart. (Comparison with contemporaneous Anglo-Saxon songs is as a rule specious, of little interest, but there is food for thought in the fact that a few months before Brassens was urging his heroine to 'Passe-les tous par tes charmes' the up-and-coming young Cliff Richard was singing of his sinister intention to 'lock up' his 'living doll' in 'a trunk'...).

    Women's sexuality is also somewhat surprisingly emphasised in those pieces most reminiscent of traditional French folk song. While some eighteenth-century *chansons de gaillard* euphemistically evoke lost honour in coy tales of a 'rose blanche' or an 'avantage' gone with the wind or lost at sea (*Les Filles de La Rochelle, La Danaé*) they do not hint at female complicity, tending rather to feature seduced and desperate maidens. More generally, the shepherdesses *et al.* of the French popular song are modest or naïve ('Ne rougis pas', the heroine of *Il pleut, il pleut, bergère* or *La*

Hospitalité is enjoined), the wives whose husbands are at war are steadfast and faithful. Of Brassens' 'blonde' in *La Route aux quatre chansons* we may learn that 'Avec elle, sous l'édredon, / Il y avait du monde', but her prototype loves her 'joli mari' and would give Touraine, Paris, Saint-Denis etc. to have him back. Brassens also causes his naked *baigneuse* in *Dans l'eau de la claire fontaine* (indissociable to all Francophone audiences from her who bathes *A la claire fontaine*) to stretch out arms and tender lips to her enchanted Galahad — and to pray for gusts of wind to enliven future ablutions. Vassal has emphasised the 'érotisme très franc' of *La Chasse aux papillons* wherein, although both lovers have 'un volcan dans l'âme', her suitor's affectionate embrace ('il se fit tendre') would appear much less passionate than Cendrillon's reaction, which has 'sa bouche en feu' (*82*, p.30). Finally the brazen Clairette admits to slipping the fateful ant down her ruffle precisely in order to encourage investigation into its whereabouts. (Given the above selected examples might one in retrospect be tempted to regard the inexplicable swinging open of the gorilla's cage as the work of (all too) human agency ...?)

Overtly sexual references colour, but do not necessarily dominate, the numerous pieces that can be termed love-songs. Frequently the heroines of these are anonymous, ageless, less individualised than symbolic of a specific moment or happening in a (male) life: the sharing of an umbrella, the loss of virginity, abandonment, a storm, the resented healing of a broken heart, etc. In one noteworthy case (*Saturne*; see below), however, the woman is plainly not young — which serves to illustrate and introduce a second aspect of Brassens' work usefully highlighted: the attention, sexual or otherwise, it pays to older women.

Brassens' most celebrated female senior citizen is the 'centenaire' whose demeanour doubtless contributed to the initial banning from the airwaves of *Le Gorille*. She alone of the female witnesses of the animal's escape does not panic, finding the possibility of exciting his ardour 'inespéré'. Bestiality aside, it should be noted that the narrator on two occasions reinforces the link between the old lady and sexual activity, once by revealing that, should he himself ever face the gorilla's dilemma 'C'est, j'en suis convaincu, la vieille / Qui sera l'objet de mon choix', and again

when imputing his own preference 'd'opter pour la vieille' to anyone
in this novel situation. A less well-known centenarian is similarly
linked to matters sexual, this time with the added taboo of incest, by
those 'sal's types' *Les Voisins*. Deeming suspect the penchant of the
narrator's grandmother for visiting her grandson these neighbours
spread the rumour that he is 'un affreux pervers, / Un incestueux
garnement / Qui couche avec sa grand-maman.' And while this
particular grandchild would appear to be the victim of gross slander,
the protagonist of the unrecorded *Le Petit-fils d'Œdipe* is sufficiently
comfortable with his taboo relationship to confound his irate father
with a supremely tasteless, lightning-fast quip that is of course an
irreproachable alexandrine: '" — T'as baisé ma maman, petit
énergumène". / " — T'avais qu'à commencer par pas baiser la
mienne"'. It is worth mentioning finally that *Le Fantôme*'s
centuries-old heroine leads her appreciative lover to claim that most
of the 'belles dames de jadis' (by definition 'old') are 'Plus expertes
dans le déduit' than many of their living (younger) counterparts ...

Ribaldry notwithstanding, the older woman has a major role in
two 'portrait songs' that are amongst Brassens' best-known. *Jeanne*
is the strongly autobiographical and idealised tribute to the sometime
lover and lifelong friend, thirty years Brassens' senior, with whom
he lodged for more than two decades. In it a personage most
witnesses describe as temperamental, possessive and on occasion
violent (*7*, p.79; *4*, p.47) becomes hospitality personified, a 'mère
universelle', essentially a white-haired fairy godmother. Interestingly, the vocabulary and imagery place this piece in the world of the
magic and the marvellous — of the fairy tale. It is the wolf trying to
dupe the kids into opening their door who shows the 'patte blanche'
in an effort to pass for their mother; it is traditionally in cabbages
and under rose bushes that babies arrive. Bread tasting like cake,
water like wine: these are reminiscent of miracles brought about *par
enchantement* in many a tale. And numerous stories tell of generous
souls sharing their last crust with strangers later revealed as
magicians or gods in disguise. Jeanne Planche, eking out rations for
two and feeding three, passionate, jealous, recklessly generous and
famously incapable of killing a pampered duck, encouraged
Brassens' work, but could not know that he would eventually be able
to repay her with a comparable generosity, ensuring Marcel's speedy

retirement, modernising and then purchasing the couple's home for so long his own. The extra-ordinary atmosphere of the song simply echoes an extra-ordinary reality.

If the life of Jeanne Planche is romanticised into that of the Old Woman Who Lived in a Shoe, the same cannot be said of the abnegation, understated, unremitting, characterising that of the unnamed 'vieille de somme', indifferent to the bitter northern wind as she collects wood for a fire for the dying Bonhomme. The incarnation of human forbearance, sorrow and love, the old woman has a universality and a greatness to which both public and critics respond unanimously. There are to be met with on occasion characters somehow too big for the specific work containing them (Annable in *The White Peacock*; Ezra Jennings in *The Moonstone*); this grave, stark tribute pushes back the frontiers of an entire genre. Great art blurs boundaries (perfect theatre, for example, can simultaneously be sublime poetry), which explains why several critics have instinctively sought to discuss *Bonhomme* in terms of its visual ('tout en demi-teinte', *3*, p.46; 'la rigueur d'un dessin à la plume', *33*, p.90), auditory ('la mélodie [qui] secoue ces strophes désolées et les fait claquer, geindre, hurler comme un vent d'hiver', *5*, p.12) or physical impact ('C'est une œuvre qui coupe le souffle [...] On en reste glacé, terrassé, on a la gorge nouée', *5*, p.12). And the emotional response is complex; pity vies with pride in human endurance and admiration, perhaps envy, at the strength of affection (lines 4 and 5 of verses one and two are the only two to contain repetition, of 'Bonhomme' and 'qu'elle aime' respectively). This is, as Brassens himself observed, a love song; it is, that is to say, a song about love. His comment that 'c'est pas triste de voir une femme qui a été trompée par un homme et qui, au moment où il va mourir, va lui chercher du bois pour le chauffer. Au contraire, c'est réconfortant, c'est une chanson d'espoir' (*21*, p.213) may initially seem to beg the question '*réconfortant* for whom?' but in fact reinforces that ambivalent compassion-admiration reaction which guarantees the work total immunity from sentimentality. Some have seen *Chanson pour l'Auvergnat* as promoting specifically Christian values (*34*, p.70), a view it is not difficult either to understand or contest. Bonhomme's old woman, symbol above all of 'la puissance, la durée, l'inviolabilité d'un véritable amour' (*33*, p.190) would seem to me to reply, in every particular, to St Paul's definition of Charity, today become Love, which 'beareth all things, believeth all things, hopeth all things, endureth all things'.

Saturne, finally, on a less solemn but a very tender note, sings the praises of an ageing but not agèd woman, like all her kind a victim (the opening conceit has it) of a humourless god's efforts to pass the time. Brassens' affection for the Middle Ages is well-documented; here, however, he leans more towards the Renaissance, concurring with Bacon's defence of mature beauty and echoing Donne: 'No spring, nor summer beauty hath such grace, / As I have seen in one autumnal face' ('The autumnal'). The loved one, constantly reassured that she is a beautiful and sought-after companion, is invited to that natural playground that is, traditionally, the garden, in order to take part in a game equally traditionally linked to the youngest of lovers, 'Loves me, loves me not'; that the couple will use for the purpose a bloom from a late, Indian summer adds a particular poignancy. The final verse makes a blessing out of familiarity, and in an extra couplet of a very different tone and register sets up a youth-maturity comparison, only to dismiss the former with unconcealed contempt. The older woman in Brassens' work and in his life — Jeanne Planche was thirty years his senior, his companion of over thirty years, Joha Heiman, ten — effortlessly eclipses younger rivals.

Final points worthy of note in any consideration of women in the Brassens canon must be (a) that the remaining two to whom an entire song is devoted are neither obviously young nor old, blond nor brunette, plump nor slender and (b) that they are defined solely in terms of their relation to men — even, in the case of the otherwise anonymous 'Femme d'Hector', in the title. The latter, 'vrai' nounou', 'fé' bienfaisante', 'divine cousette' in fact has much in common with the 'mère éternelle' 'Jeanne' (in life a dress-maker), tirelessly organising a group of non-individualised *marginaux* usually down at heel/on their luck/in the dumps, taking in hand their darning, their dying, and their disappointments in matters amatory. Most critics (*2*, p.47; *84*, p.64) concur that the description of this paragon in the last lines of the fifth verse ('Qui nous dispense sa tendresse, / Tout's ses économi's d'caresses') emphasises an unfettered and expansive nature, in Fallet's words 'au grand cœur et à la large couche' (*10*, p.84). Rioux takes refuge in citation: 'Elle est celle "qui nous saute au cou" qui nous "dispense sa tendresse"' (*15*, p.44); Calvet interestingly attempts identification: 'C'est Raymonde Laville, la femme de Victor, mais "la femme de Victor" aurait eu un pied de trop' (*7*, p.99). It certainly focuses on a wholly male 'nous' whose admiration is on the evidence proportionate uniquely to the quantity of services rendered them. Bonnafé, ordinarily so perspicacious, opines that the song offers women an ideal they must hope to emulate: 'Quel beau rêve, pour elles, que de se faire "La Femme d'Hector"' (*5*, p.23). He goes on to forestall any expression of incredulity such a claim might give rise to — 'C'est un rêve d'homme, dira-t-on' — only to plunge deeper into generalisation: 'Mais non, la générosité, la largesse, le désir de semer partout le bonheur sont bien plus naturels aux femmes, à celles qui le sont vraiment...' Self-sacrifice, we are to concur, is its own reward, at least from the female perspective. Remove the negatives from the three verbal structures in the final verse to find the other consolations proffered this indefatigable help-mate. One can but trust she will appreciate them.

In diametric opposition to Hector's wife, forever frantically active, Pénélope is static, absorbed in her needlework, hidden from view behind the curtains of a suburban villa. Strictly speaking, apart from as a perfect wife, she is hardly permitted to exist — 'l'intraitable' offers the sole swift glimpse we are given into her personality — because this dense text thenceforth takes the form of four negative questions (followed by one negative imperative) quizzing her about dreams and longings the narrator can only speculate about. Wilmet's Pénélope 'rêvant, le temps d'un soupir, à l'amour' (*23*, p.49); Sallée's: 'Elle rêve de troquer tous ses paquets d'aiguilles contre une flèche de Cupidon' (*17*, p.106) and Ghézi's 'les rêves d'une autre vie de l'épouse Pénélope' (*11*, p.103) are mere revelatory figments of those (male) critics' imaginations. In fact it adds immeasurably to the song's charm that the interrogatives convey an intrigued curiosity; in the situation of this solitary spouse, we sense, the narrator knows how *he* would feel, thinks he can imagine how *she* does, but cannot be sure. (Even the imperative of the final verse can be seen as reassuring him rather than her, the 'bored housewife' constituting a traditional male fantasy he is eager to corroborate.) His voice is indeed, as Fallet has it, 'celle de la provocation' (*10*, p.92), the which does not mean, as the selfsame writer maintains, that 'il n'est pas d'œuvre plus féministe'. There are however few as rich, as well-crafted, and demonstrating such a gift for both haunting imagery and imaginative euphemism. 'Pareille à un portrait de Vermeer de Delft' (*33*, p.90), *Pénélope* is one of the most memorable, and certainly one of the deftest, of Brassens' female portraits.

4. Chanson et langue

It is essentially to questions concerning the 'whats', 'whys' and 'whens' of a body of work — what is given prominence, lauded, reviled, omitted, ridiculed, and why it is, and why it is at that specific time — that examination of its major concerns such as that undertaken in the previous two chapters hopes to respond. Situating Brassens' songs within a socio-literary-historical framework, and then more particularly within that of *la chanson* — in other words, exploring the 'where' with regard to his *œuvre* — is equally of the essence.

French *belles-lettres*' attitude towards song is paradoxical (hence the debate over the appropriateness of awarding Brassens the 1967 Grand Prix de Poésie). On the one hand it is revered as authentic popular art of impeccable pedigree, having 'de vigoureuses et profondes racines dans le terroir et le terreau national, puisqu'à l'origine musique et poésie étant liées, tout poème était chanson et toute chanson poème' (*45*, p.467). It would also seem true to say that throughout history (and an *Histoire de la France par les chansons* of course exists (*25*)) whatever 'it' was, the French 'had a song for it' — and if they did not, an existing piece would speedily become an anthem (*Le Temps des cerises*, *Le Vieux Chalet*). On the other hand modern dictionary definitions share a clear note of disparagement: thus the *Hachette encyclopédique* glosses *chanson* as a 'petite composition chantée, de caractère populaire, au rythme simple, d'inspiration légère, sentimentale ou satirique'. (If one then looks up 'sentimental' the secondary signification, 'empreint d'une tendance à l'émotion facile, un peu mièvre', has as its illustration 'une chanson sentimentale'.) Expressions including the word again stress superficiality or limited worth: 'Chansons que tout cela!', 'Toujours la même chanson!' And Brid'oison's comment is explained as 'une allusion à la légèreté prêtée aux Français'. Is this modern ambivalence uneasily upholding the gradually widening rift the Renaissance made definite?

For in the Middle Ages, *chanson* and poetry were indeed synonymous. Troubadours offered An Entertainment centering on contemporaneous events, eulogising the famous and powerful or singing of courtly or again rustic love. To such were then added songs to be danced to (which widened audiences beyond the aristocracy), *chansons épicuriennes*, bawdy pieces that were 'rabelaisiennes avant la lettre' (*42*, p.11), and songs to work to: marching songs for crusading soldiers, and later those fighting the Hundred Years War, *chansons de toile* for the female weavers in the North, rhythmed by foot-pedal and shuttle. In the XIVth and XVth centuries song became ever more popular — and poetry became ever more subject to rules governing its structure. Fixed forms — the *virelai, triolet, rondeau* — were introduced and refined. Towards the end of the XVth century the spotlight fell with a vengeance on rhyme, and technical virtuosos delighted in mastering the latest restrictive pattern, 'rimes équivoquées, 'annexées' or tortuously 'batelées' (this last requiring the final syllable of line one to rhyme with the fourth of line two, the last of line three with the fourth of line four, etc.). Small wonder that Du Bellay was to react so strongly against poetry as a manifestation of mathematical prowess and condemn as 'épiceries' those fixed forms he saw as artificial.

As for metre, equally a question of fashion, the octosyllable of medieval narrative poems, but also of Villon's *Testament*, of the *fabliau* and again of nineteenth-century romantic verse, was and is rarely out of favour. The decasyllable was what structured *chansons de geste* but until its rehabilitation in the nineteenth century, it was thenceforth for the most part abandoned in favour of the infinite variety of the alexandrine, whose 'rythme interne [...] admet [...] 25 variations possibles' (*87*, p.31).

Brassens' passion for and impressive knowledge of the poetry of every age is well documented by numerous friends and interviewers who incorporate into their articles a brief résumé of his bookshelf contents. Villon, Régnier, Marot, Rabelais, Ronsard and also Montaigne, Voltaire, then Musset, Hugo, Lamartine, Verlaine, up to Francis Jammes, Valéry, Prévert, Paul Fort, Desnos, Aragon. So too is his interest in French folklore, in the roots of the traditional popular song, its *lieux communs*, its universality. Some of his own works contain evidence of such cultural immersion; others appear rather to be wholly permeated by it, thus seeming both timeless and a distillation of the folksongs of centuries.

Hence a piece like the plaintive octosyllabic *A l'ombre du cœur de ma mie* combines elements of folksong tradition (sleeping beloved, stolen kiss), fairy-tale (Sleeping Beauty, 'bonnes fé's', 'enchantements' and watchful birds, as in some versions of Cinderella), setting them within a verse-form favoured in medieval times and equally typically incorporating elements of repetition (cf. *Oncle Archibald, La Fille à 100 sous, L'Assassinat*). The archaic 'ma mie' and the crossbow reinforce this atmosphere, described by Fallet as 'délicatesse de tapisserie, lumière de feu de bois, frisson de brocart' (*10*, p.83). Lines 10 and 11 echo Racine (*Andromaque*), and Lucienne Cantaloube-Ferrieu stresses 'la silhouette' of the ever-present La Fontaine impressed particularly on lines 13 to 16 (*29*, p.396). I would add to the above the notion of verbal soft-filter in the form of 'l'ombre', 'faisant semblant', 'une manière de baiser', 'rumeurs', all terms which suggest rather than define, and which compliment the equally vague ending which portrays the narrator seeking either a new sweetheart... or starlings upon which to wreak vengeance.

The apostrophised sister recalls *Comme une sœur,* in which the narrator again presses his suit somewhat brusquely, this time eschewing kisses in favour of a nibble at a toe. Again this is a traditional structure of octosyllables, three of every four of which are lengthened into alexandrines by virtue of repetition of the final four syllables, with 'maroufle' in particular dating the vocabulary, and wishful thinking providing the hope but not the certainty of a satisfactory reversal of fortunes. This song also pays homage to the traditional conceit of metamorphosis, within which the human form is shed (here, the lover disguises himself as a spermwhale) in order to trick, reach or escape lover or mistress. Luc Decaunes cites one such song, dedicated to Belle Margarideto, of which verses 3 and 4 will suffice to illustrate the genre:

Alors je serai vite	– Pêcheur, tu perds ta peine,
Auprès du ruisselet:	Je glisse entre tes doigts.
Tu viens, ô Marguerite,	Fuyant à perdre haleine,
Te prendre à mon filet.	Je suis la biche au bois.

(He goes on to opine that 'tout le monde, en France', is at least familiar with the Provençale version 'O Magali ma tant amado', in which persistence does in fact reap its reward, the suitor finally being offered his beloved's ring.) And Colin Evans cites another version, 'Les Transformations', in an article (*48*) centering on *Je rejoindrai ma belle*, in which the repetition of the first two lines of each verse is echoed in both of the Brassens pieces.

Je rejoindrai ma belle shares with *A l'ombre du cœur de ma mie* its hunter, and its birds, and also incorporates a strong wind, whose presence inspires Sallée's dry observation that 'l'on songe à écrire une thèse traitant de l'influence des intempéries sur le comportement des amoureux dans l'œuvre de Brassens'. In fact inclement weather disturbing but also enhancing lovers' trysts is a traditional theme, and one Brassens exploits in *Le Chapeau de Mireille, L'Orage* — and in *Dans l'eau de la claire fontaine*. This piece lightens the tone of the Franco-Canadian lament it instantly brings to mind (*A la claire fontaine*), replacing its abandoned maiden with an opportunist naiad and its bouquet with a single rose, and giving no guarantee that the prayed-for wind will in fact return. It is also one of several songs whose heroine sports (if not for long) 'cotillon', 'corsage', 'collerette' and on occasion clogs (*Brave Margot, Clairette et la fourmi, La Chasse aux papillons, Les Amours d'antan, Je suis un voyou, Les Sabots d'Hélène*) and is more often than not a shepherdess (thus giving rise to a hitherto unsingularised offence: the 'crime de lèse-bergerette').

'On le devine', runs an observation by 'Serge' of *Les Nouvelles littéraires*, 'fort proche, par instants, ce balladin de terroir, des ménestrels qui allaient jadis de villages en châteaux' (*61*). And if this is indeed the case, it is not solely due to the setting of *La Ballade des dames du temps jadis* to music, nor to liberal references to petticoats, fountains, fairytales (*29*, pp.395-96) and folksong (*La Route aux quatre chansons, Les Sabots d'Hélène*). Nor is it attributable to titles harking back (sometimes in name alone; neither *La Ballade des cimetières* nor that of 'des gens nés quelque part' replies to either definition of the form, *87*, pp.112-13) to the traditional *supplique, complainte, ronde, blason* or *testament*. It is rather that Brassens was alone among his contemporaries in tapping into a common cultural legacy and imposing upon a distant, on one level mythical time and society a world view and set of values reinforced with each 'jadis' and 'naguère'. And it is that to which an audience responds.

Cantaloube-Ferrieu has expressed admirably the way a climate of receptivity is created, stressing 'la création délibérée, par le rapprochement d'éléments divers, d'un substrat culturel sur lequel reposent ses chansons et s'établit une complicité affective et intellectuelle avec le public' (*29*, p.394). The members of that public thus find themselves in what is both a familiar landscape, and one from which modern distractions are absent and essential truths / values/priorities unobscured. These latter can include morals in the manner of Jean de La Fontaine: 'Don't judge by appearances' (*Les Sabots d'Hélène*); 'Love hurts' (*A l'ombre du cœur de ma mie*); 'Gather ye rosebuds' (*La Chasse aux papillons*). But it is for example in *La Messe au pendu*, whose rough-justice gallows bespeak times past, and indeed only in this song, that Brassens allows himself a 'Mort à toute peine de mort!' The universal symbols of life that are fire and bread, together with the use of such words as 'croquants', 'festin' and 'huche', place *Chanson pour l'Auvergnat* in another time — and stress the sacred nature of hospitality, much-prized and sung in the Middle Ages. *Le Petit Joueur de flûteau,* of which G. Bloch wrote that '[ce] n'est qu'une gentillette médiévalerie' (*66*, p.2) while Vassal (*82*, p.38) praises it as a 'magnifique parabole', takes a theme traditional to folksong, that of the poor musician, and embroiders upon it, much as had famously Du Bellay four centuries earlier, the virtues of knowing precisely what it is one values and remaining true to that knowledge. (It would seem that the song predates the approaches made to Brassens with reference to his possible candidacy for the Académie Française.) As for the unrecorded lament *Jean rentre au village*, with its traditional repetition and question-and-answer format, one can wonder if it were not the bald, chilling and recurrent 'Le bon Dieu n'est pas gentil' that dissuaded Brassens from presenting it to the public.

Songs such as these last also importantly make the point that if the past *à la* Brassens may on occasion resemble a bucolic theme-park, it is not without its shadows. 'Porteurs de chagrin' threaten the blue skies of *La Chasse aux papillons*. Cats are bludgeoned to death. The course of true love does not always run smooth particularly if a 'gros sac d'or' or 'triste bigot' shows an interest in your sweetheart. Shepherdesses are abandoned. Hysterical mobs carry out hangings. And with 'Pauvre Martin' the human condition is freeze-framed into a Holbein engraving or a Jacques Dubois photograph (of Les Auvergnats, 1950), the repetition of the most significant lines, and of the brief refrain, bespeaking the influence of traditional laments. That said, it is difficult to share the view of Venturini (*22*, p.117), who declares himself 'troublé' by 'la singulière parenté rythmique et métrique de *Pauvre soldat* — dont la version maritime s'intitule *Brave Marin* — avec le *Pauvre Martin* de Brassens':

Brave Marin	*Pauvre Martin*
Brave marin revient de guerre,	Avec une bêche à l'épaule,
Tout doux,	Avec, à la lèvre, un doux chant,
Tout mal chaussé tout mal vêtu	Avec, à la lèvre, un doux chant,
	Avec, à l'âme, un grand courage,
	Il s'en allait trimer aux champs!

There is here perhaps a superficial similarity but it would seem to me much more appropriate to cite in this context the quatrain, attributed to Jean de Vauzelles, accompanying the grim reaper of Holbein's 'Simulacres de la mort'. Here, surely, is 'Pauvre Martin':

> A la sueur de ton visaige,
> Tu gagnerois ta pauvre vie,
> Après long travail et usaige,
> Voicy la *mort* qui te convie.

The Renaissance saw poets begin to turn away from a form of expression regarded essentially as *passé* and *populaire*. If, in the words of Michel Beaufils, poetry 'intimement liée à la musique au moyen âge a été privée de son support musical à partir du XVIIe siècle' (*3*, p.75), it was in order to distinguish itself from what was now seen as a minor art form. This would not discourage poets of the eighteenth century from composing the texts of 'chansonnettes' (such as Fabre d'Eglantine's *Il pleut bergère ou L'Hospitalité*); Crébillon, Rousseau, La Harpe — all tried their hand at a *romance* or a *pastourelle*. But it was not in the *caveau* of the early part of the century, nor in the café-concerts of the latter, that they would be aired. Not until the nineteenth century would *poètes-chansonniers* pen musical satires on current events, simultaneously rediscovering (as were Nerval, Chateaubriand and George Sand) *la chanson folklorique*. With Pierre-Jean de Béranger, France's 'ménétrier national' for Lamartine, songwriting would once again become a *métier*, and the potential of song to make less a popular than a personal statement would be recognised and realised.

Béranger is a key figure in any consideration both of French song and of Brassens' own work and trajectory. The two have much in common. Béranger (1780-1857) began, like Brassens, by being interested in poetry, but once post-revolution France began demanding more from song than 'les maris trompés, les procureurs avides' (*26*, p.xvii), decided there was '[une] nécessité de perfectionner le style et la poésie de la chanson'. Both were approached by the Académie Française, Brassens not wishing to be put forward but pleased later to accept the Grand Prix de la Poésie, Béranger arguing that 'je tiens à ne pas enrégimenter académiquement ce petit genre, qui cessera d'être une arme pour l'opposition le jour où il deviendra un moyen de parvenir' (*41*, p.286). Both too received votes at local elections at which they were not candidates, Béranger actually being elected, and having to 'resign' from his position twice.

Their works differ in three principal respects. Béranger set his texts to existent popular melodies. He was staunchly patriotic. He also wrote, most famously, many politically inspired songs, from *Le Roi d'Yvetot* satirising the morals and ambitions of Napoléon to *L'Enrhumé* and *Le Prince de Navarre*, judged at the Restoration offensive to the king and responsible for Béranger's spending three months in jail, or *Le Sacre de Charles le simple* which contributed to a further nine-month sentence. But both came to believe that their rigorous approach to songwriting, 'cette précision de la langue', 'cette richesse des idées et des images' (*41*, p.10), could serve the cause and the reputation of the genre. And a shared outlook is often discernable in what might be termed their *chansons sociales*. Both sing often of death, funerals, society's misfits, time passing — but also have a *gaillard* streak. Béranger's *curé* ('triste et bigot', *26*, p.129), his *Jeannette* ('Jamais d'une riche soie / Son corsage n'est paré'), and Lisette ('La reine des amours / N'était qu'une grisette', *26*, p.165) would be perfectly at home in a Brassens piece. Certain of the situations Béranger envisages might seem to prepare us for the absurdity of a *Ballade des cimetières* or *Le Fantôme*. Thus *Les Deux Sœurs de charité* sees a nun and a courtisane each justifying her right to a place in heaven, the nun having helped people prepare for death while her companion proceeded in a different way altogether: 'Moi, je faisais chérir la vie'. And *Les Clefs du Paradis* shows Margot stealing the keys to heaven, letting in a Turk, a Jew, a Protestant, a pope, even Satan, the last being forgiven by God, and Saint Peter finding himself on the wrong side of closed doors as Paradise 'devient gaillard'. Certain lines even bespeak a similar talent for scene-setting: 'J'avais vingt ans, une folle maîtresse, / De francs amis et l'amour des chansons' (*41*, p.130) or image-coining: when writing his 'couplets pour le mariage à l'église de deux époux mariés depuis longtemps sans cérémonie', Béranger describes their tardy decision as the act of putting 'De l'eau bénite dans leur vin' (*41*, p.42), and one recalls how the holy water in *Tempête dans un bénitier* is turned into 'eau de boudin' for want of Latin. Serge Dillaz has concluded (a trifle clumsily) that 'la personnalité de l'auteur de *Auprès de mon arbre* prolonge celle de celui de *Mon petit coin*' (*31*, p.76); it would certainly be true to say that both rejected a society's constraints and hypocrisies from a deep compassion for those whom society itself rejected.

Béranger cleared a path, as it were, for others who would become major figures in nineteenth-century *chanson*. Brassens certainly knew the work of the man thought of as Béranger's natural successor, because he recorded his *Le Roi boiteux* and *Carcassonne*. Gustave Nadaud, for a long time the only *chansonnier* to compose his own music, also wrote *Le Soldat de Marsala* with its refrain of 'Ah! que maudite soit la guerre' and *Les Deux Gendarmes,* apparently banned for the crime of 'lèse-maréchaussée'. From Jean Richepin's *La Chanson des gueux* Brassens took 'Philistins' and 'Les Oiseaux de passage', which had earned their author a fine and a month's imprisonment. He also recorded four songs by Aristide Bruant.

Black hat, black suit, red scarf, Bruant, immortalised in Toulouse Lautrec's posters, sang the working-class districts of Paris (the rue St Vincent, the boulevard Richard Lenoir, the Bastille) — their inhabitants, their streets, their stories. His *chansons naturalistes*, anticlerical, deriding the bourgeois, champion *midinettes*, unmarried mothers, gangsters, prostitutes ('On m'app'lait mam' la colonelle, / A Grenelle'), all in heavy Parisian slang. Bruant was himself a gifted showman and an excellent businessman from a middle-class family from the Loire. There is a superficial resemblance between some of his songs and some of Brassens' (*Les Amours d'antan*, *Le Mauvais Sujet repenti*, *Les Ricochets*, *La Complainte des filles de joie*, *Embrasse-les tous*) concerned with Paris, women of easy virtue, or both, but there the resemblance ends. Tone and language are very different, and so too is the portrayal, Brassens' main characters remaining with one, vivid, individualised, Bruant's blurring into a composite 'apache', orphan or prostitute.

In fact if Brassens seems in any way to echo any of Béranger's immediate successors it is because his work has something of what G. Joly has called 'la verve dure d'un Gaston Couté' (*53*). The 'dénonciation des gros propriétaires terriens [...] dégoût de la prostitution et de l'amour réduit, par les nantis, au rang de marchandise [...] sens aigu de la liberté individuelle, rejet d'une religion ne prônant plus qu'une charité de façade [...] antimilitarisme virulent' characteristic of Couté (*39*, p.791) fuel *Pauvre Martin*, *Les Croquants*, *La Complainte des filles de joie*, *La Mauvaise Réputation*, *Mourir pour des idées*, *Les Deux Oncles*, etc. Brassens seems to share, with his Fossoyeur, something of Couté's wry humour as demonstrated in *Le Champ de naviots*:

> Et tertous, l'pèsan coumme el'riche,
> El'rich tout coumme el' pauv' pèsan,
> On les a mis à plat sous l'friche;
> C'est pus que du feumier à pesant,
> Du bon feumier qu'engraiss' ma tarre
> Et rend meilleurs les vins nouvieaux :
> V'là c'que c'est qu' d'êt' propriétare
> D'eun' vigne en cont' el' champ d'naviots!

(*37*, p.85)

And first cousin to the heroine of *A l'eau de la claire fontaine*, Couté's *Casseuse de sabots* repeatedly breaks her clogs in order to have an excuse to visit the clog-maker. There is also something in *La Guerre de 14-18* that echoes the irony of *Le Gâs qu'a perdu l'esprit*, in which the titular 'gâs' spouts unpalatable truths to a variety of characters (a bourgeois, a 'gros vicaire', the Mayor) including a 'bieau militaire'— 'Je mourrons ben sans qu'on nous tue!' — and causes the narrator to hazard that, should Christ return to that time and society, 'Pas mal de gens dirin de lui: / "C'est un gâs qu'a perdu l'esprit!"'

With the twentieth century, the *chanson de charme* would rival *la chanson naturaliste*; the music-hall would make and break stars (Chevalier, Mistinguett, Fréhel), jazz would arrive from the USA; Vincent Scotto would write over four thousand songs. Piaf would sing the seedy underbelly of Paris, Trenet the joy of the sun-filled 'routes de France', and Mireille and Jean Nohain bring a welcome twist of wit and irony. Georges Brassens never tired of stressing that he was born into a family that sang, continually; he retained, effortlessly, words and music of an impressive number of the songs of his youth, astonishing Mireille during the 'Grand Echiquier' Jacques Chancel dedicated to her with his memory for the words of songs she herself had forgotten writing. With Sève, he is categorical: 'tout m'a influencé [...] moi je peux dire qu'enfant, rien de ce qui était musique ne m'était étranger. Je n'avais qu'un critère: une certaine émotion' (*18*, pp.18–19). His eclectic choice both of reading and of listening material informs his unique *œuvre*. Added to which, as Guller has it, 'Il a fallu des siècles de littérature, tout autant que de chanson et de langue parlée [...] pour produire ces architectures d'une arachnéenne puissance' (*33*, p.96).

'Y mettre du Brassens'

Of interest and relevance though they doubtless are, a familiarity with Brassens' favoured themes, or again an understanding of the musical tradition with which he aligned himself, do not in themselves suffice to explain either his originality or his appeal. It is *how* he chooses to present a given idea or subject and the specific treatment given it — what, precisely, he does to 'y mettre du Brassens' — that it is of the essence to examine.

A consummate wordsmith, Brassens plays knowledgeably and affectionately with language, his obvious enjoyment of a particularly well-turned expression, racy image or pointed reference transferring itself to his public and simultaneously heightening his audience's own appreciation of his erudition and invention. Contrast, for example, is an effect he particularly favours. Friends have commented upon the pleasure he took in mixing registers: 'Il s'en fallut de peu qu'elle ne la rendît nase', Mario Poletti recalls his commenting on the return of a loaned car and again, to a hotel worker asked to hurry along awaited companions: 'Auriez-vous pour agréable de demander à nos femmes si elles ne nous prennent pas pour des cons' (*84*, p.38). Similarly, Oncle Archibald dies 'En courant sus à un voleur / Qui venait de lui chiper l'heure', the first verb imparting a highly literary flavour to his attack while 'chiper' returns us to a much more familiar register. The infamous gorilla is transformed in the space of four lines from a 'singe en rut' escaping his cage; 'le quadrumane accéléra / Son dandinement', the song continues, with multisyllabic precision. And the choice of expression of another protagonist underlines the bitterness of the spurned lover: 'Parlez-moi d'amour et j'vous fous mon poing sur la gueule, / Sauf le respect que je vous dois.'

On occasion the contrast operates on the form/content level; thus for example *Stances à un cambrioleur*, *A l'ombre des maris* and *La Fessée* all discuss the morally questionable ('Avez-vous remarqué que j'avais un beau cul?') in alexandrines. On occasion, too, the musical accompaniment offsets intrinsically sober topics. The refrain of *Les Funérailles d'antan* is at the very least irreverent; *Grand-père* clip-clops gaily along despite the delay to a burial it describes. Particularly worthy of note is *Tempête dans un bénitier*, whose refrain is given over to an élite amateur choir made up of Brassens' close friends, and which uses a particular sprightly rhythm and vulgar vocabulary — 'les fidèl's s'en foutent', 'ces putains / De moines qu'ils nous emmerdent' — to lament the passing of the Latin mass.

There are also several songs whose ending or *chute* contrasts strongly with what precedes it. Each verse of *Le Vingt-deux septembre* catalogues the past suffering of an abandoned lover but ends 'aujourd'hui, je m'en fous' — time, we take it, has healed the broken heart. But the five *sixains* are followed by a single, wistful alexandrine, 'Et c'est triste de n'être plus triste sans vous', whose double-take melancholy pulls one up short. The lamenting of 'le joli temps des coudé's franches' of *Le Père Noël et la petite fille* has already been discussed. And perhaps most trenchantly, *Le Sceptique*'s seven verses confidently proclaim the narrator's uniform dismissal of systems of faith, divination, absolute proof, the efficacy of the death penalty, the glorifying of the dead and the sacrificing of lives for a putative glowing future ... but then reveals the sensitivity to the comforts of belief: 'Mais j'envie les pauvres d'esprit pouvant y croire.'

Brassens' vocabulary, most thoroughly analysed in Hantrais's study, reveals certain characteristics in particular which contribute to the distinctive style and myth that is his. Most noticeable is his use of nouns relating to a bygone age ('calèche', 'maroufle', 'manant', 'maraud', 'chaumine' are a few examples). This 'age' is non-specific and not necessarily consistent for the duration of a song; Comay has pointed out that '"botillon" (mot apparu en 1940 nous dit le Petit Robert) est anachronique en regard de "quenouille"' (*9*, p.11). But it is always a pre-electricity, pre-television age of clog-wearers and coalmen, a world evocative of many traditional songs, and one only Brassens of his contemporaries sought to exploit.

For the most part reinforcing such vocabulary are the numerous references to figures biblical, literary or mythological. These may be familiar, such as *L'Assassinat*'s 'pauvre comme Job', several references to Cupid, and the use of the Greek or Roman goddess of love as a kind of shorthand to symbolise beauty and physical attraction. But, as Hantrais points out, even when they are not, such references appear 'dans des contextes qui exploitent leurs associations et qui les rendent évidentes dans le cas où elles auraient pu être obscures' (*12*, p.193). A case in point occurs for example in *Le Cocu*, where the learned reference — 'Cocu, tant qu'on voudra, mais pas amphitryon'— is almost instantly glossed: 'Partager sa moitié, est-c' que cela comporte / Que l'on partage aussi la chère et la boisson?'

If Brassens on occasion introduces a word likely to cause most listeners to consult a dictionary ('lustral', 'callipyge', 'l'autan') he is similarly at pains to enrich certain texts with choice slang. Calvet has consulted books from Brassens' own collection and gives a glimpse of the research constantly undertaken: 'Dans un dictionnaire d'argot, *L'Argot en cinq sec*, il entoure des mots ("cogne", "fiole") et surtout des expressions ("avoir la dalle en pente", "avoir la fièvre de bercy")' (*7*, p.61). In *La Complainte des filles de joie* is a case in point: 'La noce est jamais pour leur fiole' immediately precedes 'Fils de pécore et de minus, / Ris pas de la pauvre Vénus'. Here the first line mimics that most celebrated of descriptions of Phèdre, 'la fille de Minos et de Pasiphaé', while the second effects an ellipsis of the first element of the negative imperative as is common in spoken French and incorporates 'Vénus' as (common enough) synonym for prostitute. The erudite allusion and the colloquial structure combine much as do the mixes of actual register mentioned above.

Brassens' penchant for sharp contrasts and a specific and rich vocabulary complement another trait that is arguably his most distinguishing stylistic feature. Wilmet terms 'maximes rénovés' (*23*, p.60), Beaufils 'l'éclatement de formules toutes faites' (*3*, p.34), Vassal 'le détournement d'expressions idiomatiques' (*21*, p.141) and Comay simply 'son procédé' (*9*, p.77) a rejuvenation of (for the most part) an idiom by replacing an element of it with a new term giving an entirely new slant to the expression. This operation is most usually performed on nouns: thus for example on the model of 'mener quelqu'un par le bout du nez', the protagonist of *Une jolie fleur* becomes one 'qui vous mène par le bout du cœur'; in *Les Deux Oncles*, Brassens coins yet another euphemism for dying — 'prendre la clé des cieux', patterned after 'prendre la clé des champs' — which becomes 'la clef du champ de navets' in *Le Revenant*; in *Le Testament*, studded with such gems, '[faire] l'école buissonnière' provides the inspiration for the unforgettable 'faire la tombe buissonnière'. But verbs are not spared: the vulgar expression denigrating self-aggrandisement, 'péter plus haut que son cul', is used as the basis for an expression Oscar Wilde, dying 'beyond his means', would surely have envied ('mourir plus haut que son cul'); the general notion of doing something behind somebody's back, 'faire quelque chose sur l' dos de quelqu'un', is given a specificity in

Le Fossoyeur (it is so often to death that these reworked expressions
refer) whose soft-hearted hero regrets having to 'gagner son pain sur
le dos des morts'; and *Le Bulletin de santé* sees stories 'à dormir
debout' transformed into 'des contes à mourir debout'. Past
participles, finally, are on occasion exploited: 'recevoir quelqu'un à
bras ouverts' gives rise in *Grand-père* to the eloquent 'Le marchand
nous reçut à bras fermés'; the notion of attacking someone 'à bras
raccourcis' inspires in *La Ronde des jurons* that of swearing 'à
langue raccourci'' and the image of racing flat out, 'à bride abattue',
inspires that of the obliging narrator of *Le Bulletin de santé*,
'servicing' journalists' wives (amongst others) 'à fesses rabattu's'.

On occasion an expression offers such rich pickings that
Brassens exploits it more than once. Prudent advice to those likely to
speak first and think later, 'il faut tourner sept fois sa langue dans sa
bouche avant de parler', becomes in *Le Vin* 'tourner sept fois sa
langue dans sa gueule de bois'; stretched to accommodate not only
words but actions, it reappears in *Les Deux Oncles* as 'tourner sept
fois sa crosse dans la main'. Similarly 'suivre son petit bonhomme
de chemin', a common locution conveying the notion of 'going
along one's own sweet way', is restructured into literal description in
La Mauvaise Réputation — 'suivre son chemin de petit bonhomme'
— and returned to in *Pénélope* where the protagonist is pictured
following her 'petit bonhomme de bonheur', the which offers an
original picture of the limits of domestic contentment. And at other
times it is an expression's potential to be mined for both literal and
figurative signification simultaneously that is revealed; thus of the
sentimental oak in *Le Grand Chêne* we learn that 'bien qu'il fût en
bois, les chênes, c'est courant / La fable ne le laissait pas
indifférent', and of the 'gens nés quelque part' that 'c'est pas un lieu
commun celui de leur naissance'.

The effect of most of Brassens' word-play is humorous. But
equally, if *Celui qui a mal tourné* escapes being mawkish, it is to a
large extent due to such turns of phrase as that explaining that the
narrator is sent 'à la Santé / [Se] refaire une honnêteté', as though the
experience of imprisonment somehow paralleled that of those
convalescing 'pour se refaire une santé'. And if the notion of 'seeing
someone coming a mile off' ('avec ses gros sabots') is made to refer

to ideas apparently worth dying for, incorporating a sideswipe at fanatical patriotism is particularly pointed:

> Mourir pour des idé's, c'est bien beau, mais lequelles?
> Et comme toutes sont entre elles ressemblantes,
> Quand il les voit venir, avec leur gros drapeau,
> Le sage, en hésitant, tourne autour du tombeau.

As indeed is the appropriation of the traditional children's song (*Ainsi font, font, font les petites marionnettes*) in *Les Deux Oncles,* wherein are represented ideas 'qui viennent et qui font / Trois petits tours, trois petits morts, et puis s'en vont'. Such turns of phrase, characteristic of Brassens, can thus serve both as aural italicisation of important points, and as leaven to lighten tone.

What of certain other stylistic effects found less frequently but equally memorably in the Brassens canon? The wry litotes serves essentially to underline some human absurdity: thus the narrator of *Les Funérailles d'antan* assures us that, rather than settling for a simple, straightforward funeral, 'J'aim'rais mieux mourir dans l'eau, dans le feu, n'importe où, / Et même, à la grand' rigueur, ne pas mourir du tout.' The apostrophe in *Le Gorille* both continues the suspense and achieves the verbal equivalent of a change in camera angle, inviting the listener to take part in the song by eliciting his opinion; that of *Les Amours d'antan*, on the other hand, echoing Villon's balder 'Prince', helps to establish and maintain a particular atmosphere ('Mon prince, on a les dam's du temps jadis qu'on peut'). Antiphrasis and/or the exploitation of 'adjectifs impertinents' (*12*, p.167) have a comic effect ('maccabées prospères', 'putains de moines', 'fesses impies' and the celebrated neologism 'mégères gendarmicides'). Periphrasis too is often used for its humorous potential. *Le Mauvais Sujet repenti*'s definition of procuring — 'l'métier de cocu systématique' — the entire first verse of *Le Fantôme*, the second of *Le Cocu*, both illustrate this, and to justify Hantrais's observation that 'la tendance de Brassens à exagérer [...] sert toujours d'aide à la compréhension'. Other examples are more *tour de force* than comic diversion. *Le Testament* piles up near-synonyms:

> S'il faut aller au cimetière,
> J'prendrai le chemin le plus long,
> J'ferai la tombe buissonnière,
> J'quitterai la vie à reculons ...
> [...]
> Par le chemin des écoliers

as does *La Maîtresse d'école*:

> Un baiser pour de bon, un baiser libertin,
> Un baiser sur la bouche, enfin bref, un patin,
> Enfin bref, un patin.

And *La Supplique* offers a striking original euphemism:

> Note ce qu'il faudrait qu'il advînt de mon corps,
> Lorsque mon âme et lui ne seront plus d'accord
> Que sur un seul point: la rupture.

as does *Le Mauvais Sujet repenti* with its 'endroit où le dos / R'ssemble à la lune'.

Language condensed, stretched; novel images coined, old ones pressed into new service; expressions submitted to a 'remixing' — Brassens' early interest in Surrealist experimentation with language (evident from his novel *La Tour des miracles*) is reflected by the way he seems to make words jump through new hoops, breathing life into stale adages while creating new clichés ('une jolie fleur dans une peau d'vache') for his time. Bonnafé has written that an examination of his style 'révélerait très bien son désir de tout mettre sens dessus dessous'. Certainly even the briefest of analyses points up a determination to hammer language into precisely the form (and the timbre, and the style) required for each of the deliberately crafted statements that are his songs.

It would seem pertinent to conclude this chapter with a short investigation of the controversy, mentioned in the introduction, that accompanied the awarding to Brassens of the Académie Française's Grand Prix de Poésie, if only because it is an intrinsically gallic *guerre de plume* whose object must have drawn considerable satisfaction from the position it placed him in.

A matter of weeks after the prize was announced *Le Magazine littéraire* in the shape of Jean Patrick Maury asked the question 'Brassens est-il un poète?' and concluded: 'Artisan du verbe. Mais que l'on me pardonne si je n'escamote pas tout à fait ce sentiment: Baudelaire, Rimbaud, Eluard, eux, étaient des poètes' (*78*, p.30). A few months later Robert Poulet, unashamedly provocative, wondered how the Académie could thus distinguish 'je ne sais quel chanteur, auteur de strophes et d'apostrophes au dessous du médiocre' (*46*). And on Brassens' death Alain Bosquet reiterated and developed his argument of fourteen years previously: 'privés de leur musiquette, ses textes sont des platitudes, indignes d'être lues' (*80*).

Brassens himself avoided referring to his work as poetry and his interviews are littered with disclaimers: 'des strophes! Appelons-les plus modestement des couplets', his modesty on occasion deliberately excessive: 'On peut être nul, être à peu près analphabète, mais avoir le don de mettre les quatre ou cinq syllabes qu'il faut sur les quatre ou cinq bonnes notes' (*1*, p.183). But he was equally at pains to stress that it was above all his literary heritage that he drew on for inspiration and for guidance. His occasionally cavalier attitude to prosody is a case in point, an example of those liberties taken only by those thoroughly conversant with the intricacies and demands of versification. Chabrol has written of time spent dissecting acknowledged masters: thus 'nous décortiquions Aragon qui nous démontrait enfin que le nombre des rimes est illimité, puisqu'il suffit de casser les mots en bout de ligne' (*89*, no page nos, 3 from end). And how many commentators have delighted in 'Plus jamais tu n'auras à cour- / ber la tête' (*Oncle Archibald*), 'J'suis issu de gens / Qui étaient pas du gen- / re sobre' (*Le Vin*), or 'Le métier de femme ne nou-/rrit plus son homme' (*Concurrence déloyale*)?

Certainly Brassens had and has enough champions never to have needed to defend in person his award or his work. As early as 1963 Michel Perrin was exulting that '*réduits à l'état de poèmes*' (*67*, my italics), 'la plupart des chansons de Brassens gardent leurs plus vives couleurs'. Commenting on the award in June 1967, René Bourdier (*76*, p.26), defining Brassens as 'par le fond et par la forme authentique serviteur de la poésie', observes that he also has 'le

malheur de chanter. Le tort d'accompagner ses poésies de quelques
notes de musique qui font d'elles des chansons'. (He goes on to
comment that the runner-up, Frances de Dalmatie, does not sing;
'Est-elle meilleur poète pour cela?') The address by the Académie's
René Clair on the occasion of the 1967 'séance publique annuelle'
quotes *Supplique* and then observes 'C'est trahir ce poète que de
citer ses vers dépouillés de leur mélodie. Non pas qu'à être lus ils
perdent l'âpreté de leur charme ou l'humour qui éclaire leur
mélancolie, mais parce que c'est le rythme musical qui y impose et
gouverne élisions, enjambements, brisures des mots, rimes dis-
sonantes et autres licences savoureuses sous lesquelles se devine une
parfaite connaissance du métier' (*79*).

The dispute, furthermore, has elsewhere been widened to set
song and poetry in general on opposite sides of an elaborately
constructed fence. Seghers' decision to include Aznavour, Brel and
Leclerc in its 'Poètes d'aujourd'hui' series prompted Claude Sarraute
to ask 'Si la poésie faite pour être chantée reste poésie quand elle est
lue' (*70*). She goes on to distinguish between the writing of song and
that of poems, the creative act required for the first seen as having
'absolument rien à voir' with that demanded by the second. And Jean
Clouzet's introductory essay to one of the volumes in question, that
devoted to Brel, throws down a gauntlet with the opening sentence of
what is essentially a very spirited harangue of some five pages: 'Il
est certain que faire naître une chanson est intrinsèquement plus
délicat qu'écrire un poème. Aussi tyrannique que soit l'architecture
de celui-ci, elle atteindra rarement la complexité qui préside à
l'élaboration d'une vraie chanson' (*86*). (Wilmet's chapter
'L'écrivain semi-officiel' looks more impartially at this issue, *23*,
pp.67-73.) The measured tones, and indeed the eloquence, of André
Wyss take us to the heart of the matter: 'La poésie de Brassens existe
[donc] bien, elle est cultivée, elle est savante, elle est ludique. Mais
ses visées ne sont pas strictement littéraires [...] Et il importe au
consommateur de poésie de changer ses habitudes et de se donner
toujours les moyens de sortir le poème de la page quand il s'agit
d'un texte de chanson' (*92*, pp. 86-87).

The dictionary definition cited on the opening pages of this
chapter holds a key to what is on one level a question of semantics
and connotation — and a question specific to the French language

('song' in English being defined as 'a short poem set to music or meant to be sung'). Definitions of 'chanson' are belittling and explain why one might wish to avoid such a categorisation. Furthermore the grey area between the expressive reading aloud of rhythmic writing and the singing of it similarly requires consideration, unless one wishes to raise yet another issue concerning possible differences between the poem, and 'the poem-on-the-page'. If 'poésie' is characterised by 'une utilisation des sons et des rythmes du langage (notamment dans le vers) et par une grande richesse d'images' (*Hachette encyclopédique*) it would seem churlish and indeed inaccurate to deny that poetry is what Brassens wrote — but that is only one definition. And thus I cite, to close this necessarily brief examination, a comment incidentally having much bearing on this thorny issue. George Melly, enthusing about a Beatles' classic, may be said unwittingly to have answered all those hesitant to commit themselves: 'On the written page, *Eleanor Rigby* is good minor poetry, but then it's not meant to be read but listened to and, *as a song, I believe it to be great poetry*' (*91*, pp. 79–80; my italics).

5. The Cast

'One seems always to remember them', wrote Orwell of Dickens' characters, 'doing one particular thing [...] fixed for ever like little twinkling miniatures painted on snuff-box lids, completely fantastic and incredible, and yet somehow more solid and infinitely more memorable than the efforts of serious novelists' (*90*, p.499). The observation could equally be applied to many Brassens protagonists (and on occasion to his minor characters). Thus, while listeners often retain a melody, a chorus or a favourite *gauloiserie*, they also form their own visual image as accompaniment to a song and, forgetting a title, will refer to 'the song about the bride in the ox-cart' or 'the one about the women at Brive-la-Gaillarde' (*La Marche nuptiale* and *Hécatombe* respectively).

'Toute chanson dont je ne peux pas faire une peinture ou une gouache n'existe pas pour moi', Pierre Mac Orlan was fond of saying (*34*, p.12). Recognising the visual aspect of Brassens' work, critics have mentioned Brueghel, Dubout, but also Dürer and Cézanne (Guth) in connection with it, and to date two artists, Daniel Vandendriessche and Robert Combas, have been inspired to 'translate' elected songs into paintings. And one wonders if Maxime Le Forestier's 1984 remark (*82*, p.60) that Brassens creates 'une galerie de personnages qu'on pourrait traiter en bande dessinée' was responsible for inspiring the 1989 and 1990 publications which do ... precisely that (*24*).

Aesthetic issues aside (its reception was mixed), the two-volume set, or more specifically Solé's cover for volume II, is of interest to any consideration of the Brassens cast. The illustration shows Brassens, guitar in hands, against a background of green field (complete with beaming oak) and blue sky (down from which peers a bearded head, and against which hovers a butterfly). And placed around him, proportionately about the size of his hand, are several figures. A dragoon stomps along the neck of the guitar, a gorilla barring his path and the strings. A nun stands further on, while a beclogged country maid perches revealingly below. A duck on his right sleeve inspects the scowling undertaker on his right hand; above them a disdainful fish-netted prostitute, and a tramp equipped both with bottle of wine and dainty umbrella. A policeman frowns at them from behind a lapel (the other sports a daisy). On Brassens' shoulders a priest, a blushing choirboy, a minstrel, a cat — and poised above them a smiling Cupid, arrow at the ready.

Fauna excluded, all the human characters here are instantly recognisable not as the (usually) named protagonists of the songs, but as a selection of those background characters whose recurrence confers upon them the status of symbol. The pejorative connotations of both 'caricature' and 'stereotype' mean, I think, that both terms must be rejected for these creations with which Brassens peoples the universe he shapes. They are characters in the full sense of the word; drawn in a few broad strokes, frozen in one frame (and often in one bygone age), and for all that distinctive and memorable. Erase Brassens from the Solé illustration and his world remains clearly identifiable. This is by any standard a remarkable achievement for non-visual art.

One main reason such characters endure is because they are presented as playing a part within a given event or incident of which the account becomes the song itself. A policeman dies at the end of *La File indienne*, another becoming the the hero of *L'Epave*; undertakers ruin the plans of the protagonist of *La Ballade des cimetières* and refuse to help bury Grand-père, etc. This is why they remain linked in the mind's eye to a specific act. Otherwise memorable, however, are those to whose description an entire song is devoted. The 'fille à cent sous', the depressed gravedigger, Bonhomme's wife, *Le Modeste*'s hero, Pénélope, 'la femme d'Hector', Jeanne — these are 'filled out' characters, by virtue of which fact they cannot easily be pinned down to some typical quirk. It is significantly only 'la femme d'Hector' of all these who appears in *Brassens en bande dessinée* (thirty-five songs in all being illustrated), and the figure is shown only twice from the front: complexity of character is not readily translated into visual portrait. Certainly the heroic peasant woman and maternal hostess whose door is open to all could be portrayed as archetypes, but as Marc d'Eramo has it, Brassens' characters, 'tout en étant des individus types, sont toujours des individus particuliers' (*47*, p.70). In other words, Pénélope may potentially be a bored housewife, but like Guinevere, Emma Bovary or Mrs Robinson, she will be it in an individual fashion; she is not *the* dissatisfied spouse.

For all its portrayal of the 'fine fleur de la populace' (*Le Bistrot*) and independent of the 'paysannerie intérieure' (*55*) for which it is renowned, it is undeniable that the protagonist of Brassens' work is the Brassens character himself. This personage, extravagantly described by d'Eramo as 'le seul héros entièrement positif de son monde poétique' (*47*, p.63), is both keystone and mirage (hence frequent evocations of 'the Brassens myth') and Brassens' cultivation of it as inspired a notion as that fuelling his best songs.

The quest for the origin of the Brassens persona might logically begin with an investigation of his use of the first person; at least 75% of the songs incorporate 'je'/'nous'. It is soon apparent that there are different categories, and indeed different strengths, of 'je'. There is the 'je' witness (Venturini favours 'épistolaire'; *22*, p.94) who is generally incidental to the tale told: the simple narrator (examples would be *Oncle Archibald*, *La Marguerite*). There is a 'je philosophique' who plays a far greater role in pieces that are essentially a reflection on human nature (*La Mauvaise Herbe*, *Mourir pour des idées*). A 'je' is also attributed to certain defined characters (*La Ballade des cimetière*'s collector; *Celui qui a mal tourné*) whom one would nevertheless not be tempted to confuse with their creator. And there are conflicting 'pairs': the 'je' who has found love (*Les Sabots d'Hélène*; *Saturne*) coexists with, and is far outnumbered by, the spurned or abandoned 'je' of pieces such as *Une jolie fleur* or *Les Lilas*. *Le Cocu* or *Le Pornographe*'s cuckolded 'je' is paralleled by the seducer of married women of *A l'ombre des maris* and *L'Andropause*.

These divisions are my own, and they are hesitant. Generalisation on the question is misleading: 'La plupart du temps, quand Brassens emploie le je, il pratique à la fois l'auto-ironie et l'autocritique', writes Rioux, on no obvious evidence (*15*, p.56). 'Dans douze chansons [...] on peut voir dans le *je* du conteur une projection poétisée de l'auteur' claims Hantrais. But her selection omits, for example, *Le Mécréant*, *La Non-demande en mariage*, *Le*

Moyenâgeux and *Mourir pour des idées*, which others might well consider crucial to such a list. And she cannot say more than that it is 'raisonnable de supposer' (*12*, p.107) that the chosen songs reveal Brassens' own predispositions. Furthermore Brassens himself adds to the confusion when he claims as his own sentiments he has taken care to attribute to a full-blown character : 'Je n'aime pas la mort. Je le dis nettement dans *Le Fossoyeur*: "j'ai beau m' dir' que rien n'est éternel — J'peux pas trouver ça tout naturel"' (*14*, p.59). After all, *Celui qui a mal tourné* and *La Ballade des cimetières* are written in the first person ('j'estourbis en un tournemain'; 'j'ai des tombeaux en abondance...').

And yet despite so potentially bewildering a situation the Brassens persona emerges slowly from both the work and the astonishingly rich and even lyrical press coverage it, and its intriguing creator, inspired. As d'Eramo stresses, this is nothing to do with regular evocation of 'sa pipe, ses moustaches, ses chats. Non, il s'agit d'une impression globale qui naît des vers où Brassens se dévoile, où il superpose sa propre philosophie à celle du personnage qu'il est en train de décrire' (*47*, p.63). Guy Béart is clear that it was structured: 'Il a participé à la fabrication d'un personnage pour que ça puisse porter les chansons. Puisque l'époque est comme ça' (*14*, pp.111–12). And in 1958, talking about his role as The Artist in *Porte des Lilas*, Brassens remarked to Luc Bérimont that, while audiences seemed to feel he was 'playing himself', the character 'ressemble non pas au vrai Brassens que vous connaissez mais au Brassens que le public imagine, au Brassens de la légende, au Brassens qui grogne, au Brassens qui n'aime pas les policiers, enfin au Brassens faux, qu'imagine le public [...]. C'est quelque chose d'inventé, Brassens, un peu pour le public'.[5]

Thus it becomes perfectly feasible for apparent contradictions to coexist within a construct when they would be impossible absurdities attributed to flesh and blood. Sympathy for the sadder and wiser lover whose 'jolie fleur' has terminally damaged his heart does not negate amusement provoked by *La Traitresse*'s picture of the 'cuckolded' lover whose married mistress rediscovers her husband's charm, nor prevent appreciation of the tenderness of *La*

---

[5] Interview, Luc Bérimont, Radio Nationale, 4.3.58.

Non-demande en mariage. Disbelief is suspended; Brassens becomes in turn 'Le Sceptique' and the outraged believer indignant at the demise of the Latin mass; the husband whose wife recites Claudel at intimate moments, and the harassed spouse for whom 'les joies charnelles' have lost their appeal.

Less dramatically, extremes of character, evidently Brassens' own, also contribute to the mythical persona. As prominent in his work as the 'dame de ses pensées', the 'éternelle fiancée' and the charms of 'ma mie' are the heroines of *Fernande*, *Mélanie*, *La Nymphomane* or the 'emmerderesses' of *Misogynie à part*. The disdain of *Le Pluriel* for a grouping of 'plus de quatre' coexists with the pæans to male comradeship that are *Au bois de mon cœur* and *Les Copains d'abord*.

Contrasting elements such as the above contribute much to, but alone do not define, the Brassens that emerges from the work. The repetition of anti-authoritarian, individualist sentiments, or of nostalgia for apparently kinder days, or of urging to live and let live, shape it too. As do those pieces seemingly referring directly to Brassens' life and career. Released in 1958, *Le Pornographe* wryly sums up an industry ever alert to the value of the gimmick:

> Et quand j'entonne, guilleret,
> A un patron de cabaret
> Une adorable bucolique,
> Il est mélancolique ...

And a few years on, *Les Trompettes de la renommée* catalogues tongue in cheek a variety of scandals one needing to stay in the public eye is urged to consider involving himself in 'pour les besoins d'la caus' publicitaire'. It ends, suitably, with a reaffirmation of the bearish image, of the uncompromising performer-*malgré-lui*:

> J'aime mieux m'en tenir à ma premièr' façon
> Et me gratter le ventre en chantant des chansons.
> Si le public en veut, je les sors dare-dare,
> S'il n'en veut pas je les remets dans ma guitare.
> Refusant d'acquitter la rançon de la gloir'.

There is, finally, the cumulative effect of the almost exclusively positive portrayal of 'les petits gens'. And it seems to me that what is seductive in Brassens' presentation of his 'marginaux', of the oppressed peasant or young working-class girls or spurned impoverished lovers, is partially an obvious affection (in his life, Brassens' literary and journalistic friends would rub shoulders with Marcel, who spray-painted car bodies, Jeanne, the seamstress, the postman, the housekeeper, etc.) but more an absence of pity and an admiration that does not attempt glorification (characters are not admired *despite* what they are). Absorbing such comprehensive fraternity the listener is drawn to share the laudable sentiment and admire him from whom it emanates. It is undeniably true, as Rioux has indicated, that one can perfectly well 's'apitoyer sur les misères que subit une putain mythique et mépriser sans vergogne les vraies filles qui font le trottoir rue St-Denis' (*5*, p.70). But since Brassens' songs freeze their narrator (him) in the former attitude, it is that attitude which comes to characterise and define him.

Were proof needed of the extent to which Georges Brassens was confused with the Brassens persona, the press coverage of his death, and of its tenth anniversary, certainly provides it. Journalists ransacked the work for *mots justes*: 'Nous avons tous les larmes d'Hélène' proclaimed *France-Soir* (Thierry Desjardins). 'Il s'est fait tout petit pour partir au bout de son petit bonhomme de chemin' laboured the *Parisien Libéré*; while *Le Matin*, in an attempt to out-Brassens Brassens, took inspiration from *Les Trompettes de la renommée* ('Serein, contemplatif, ténébreux, bucolique...') and summed him up as 'Discret, pudique, massif, rugueux'. Image and individual were as ever fused.

It is interesting, if of necessity inconclusive, to consider why this persona as sketched out above should have proved so popular for so long. Christophe Pinet has proposed an explanation for the early enthusiasm, positing that, by stressing the right not to choose (in for example *Les Deux Oncles* and *Mourir pour des idées*) Brassens 'offers a kind of solace to those who had to live through the occupation while agonizing over whether or not they should have taken sides' (*49*, p.281). But the reaction to such pieces was, as we have seen, in many quarters exceedingly negative. Marc Robine (*82*, p.26) stresses that 'cette image un peu caricaturale de râleurfrondeur-mauvaise-tête-mais-bon-cœur-et-grand-bouffeur-de-flics' is an image of themselves with which the French are pleased to concur. And Colin Evans adds that they identify readily with 'this non-conformist who uses the whole range of their language [...] who is strong and tender, violent and gentle, sexually vigorous but romantically ensnared' (*48*, p.676).

There is some truth in each analysis, all of which stress that public identification with the Brassens persona is what most contributed to the popularity of man and work. I would suggest in addition that a punning people with a richly homonymic language and a history of pride in its *belles lettres* responds not only to themes in Brassens' work but also to particularly original *tournures*, striking images or racy rhyme, enjoying them with a kind of linguistic gourmandise.

In Brassens' lifetime, Guy Béart has suggested, 'le personnage' was 'plus fort que l'œuvre' (*14*, pp.111-12). Now 'l'œuvre prend sa revanche'. Certainly the recent tributes (Renaud's and Maxime Le Forestier's devoting of an album each to Brassens songs, Joël Favreau uniting an impressive cast for a further recording) would seem to bear out the judgement. Deprived of its creator-*interprète* the work holds its own. More — it inspires other creators both to write songs and to interpret those of Brassens. Often their renderings ensure that the work is enriched, that nuances are exploited, that its sound is renewed, modernised. Because of this; because, too, of the universality of his themes and the variety of his treatments of them, Brassens is, and may remain longer than we could possibly have imagined, a seminal figure who is also our contemporary.

Brief Biographical Table

1921	Georges-Charles Brassens born 22nd October at Sète.
1936	Alphonse Bonnafé arrives at the Collège de Sète; inspires him to take an interest in poetry.
1939	Incident (recalled in *Les Quatre Bacheliers*) in which Brassens receives a short suspended sentence for theft.
1940	Brassens goes to Paris where he stays with his aunt and works at the Renault plant. Begins a programme of self-education, plundering the library of the XIVth arrondissement.
1942	Accepted into the SACEM (Société des auteurs, compositeurs et éditeurs de musique) as lyricist. Publishes at own expense slim volume of poetry (*A la Venvole*).
1943	Called up for Service du Travail Obligatoire and sent to Basdorf.
1944	Granted leave, fails to return, and is taken in by Jeanne and Marcel Planche, impasse Florimont.
1945	Writes for *Le Libertaire* (anarchist journal).
1947	Publishes at own expense second collection of poetry, *La Lune écoute aux portes*. Meets Joha Heiman ('Püppchen'), his companion until his death.
1948	Begins trying to place songs.
1952	6th March: is introduced to Patachou. 9th, appears at Chez Patachou. Taken on by Jacques Canetti of Les Trois Baudets and Philips. Two 78 (rpm)s recorded.
1953	Accepted into SACEM as composer. First 33 (rpm). Publishes only novel, *La Tour des miracles*. Tours

(Brussels). Meets lifelong friend novelist René Fallet. By autumn, heads the bills at Bobino.

1954   Is awarded the Grand Prix for a first album by the Académie Charles Cros. Publishes song and poetry collection *La Mauvaise Réputation*. Pierre Nicolas, a double-bass player, begins what will henceforth be his career: accompanying Brassens.

1955   Europe 1 is launched, and dares to play *Le Gorille* on air.

1956   Role of the artist in René Clair's film *Porte des Lilas*. Pierre Onteniente, met at Basdorf, becomes personal assistant (another lifetime job).

1957   Plays at Olympia, Alhambra, Bobino.

1962   At Bobino and Olympia, celebrates ten years as a performing artist. Death of mother.

1963   Emergency operation on kidneys. Seghers publishes a selection of his lyrics, prefaced by Bonnafé, in its 'Poètes d'aujourd'hui' series.

1965   Death of father and of Marcel Planche.

1967   Académie Française awards him its Grand Prix de Poésie. Jeanne Planche remarries. Brassens leaves the impasse Florimont.

1968   Death of Jeanne Planche.

1969   Selected pieces by Brassens set for some competitive examinations.

1972   Publishes *Poèmes et chansons*. Celebrates a twenty-year career. Philips issue a commemorative compilation.

1974   Achieves an entry in the *Petit Larousse* ('Brassens, Georges, chanteur français né à Sète en 1921. Auteur de chansons poétiques, pleines de verve et de non-conformisme').

1975   Grand Prix de la Ville de Paris.

1977   Last concert (Bobino).

1979   Prix du Disque de l'Académie du Disque Français.

1980   Undergoes further surgery.

1981   29th October. Dies at Saint-Gély-du-Fesc shortly after sixtieth birthday.

Select Bibliography

Place of publication Paris unless otherwise indicated. Details of currently available collections of the texts of Brassens' songs are given in the Prefatory Note. Also of interest: Brassens' one novel *La Tour des miracles*, Editions Jeunes Auteurs Réunis (1953), then Stock (1968); and a further collection of selected texts, incorporating a mini-scenario/playlet, *La Mauvaise Réputation*, Denoël (1954) then Gallimard, coll. Folio (1986).

BOOKS ON BRASSENS

1. P. Barlatier et M. Monestier, *Brassens, le livre du souvenir*, Tchou (1982), Sand (1998).
2. Michel Barlow, *Chansons de Georges Brassens*, Hatier, coll. Profil d'une œuvre (1981).
3. Michel Beaufils, *Brassens, poète traditionnel*, Imbert-Nicholas (1976).
4. Pierre Berruer, *Georges Brassens, la marguerite et le chrysanthème*, Presses de la Cité (1981).
5. Alphonse Bonnafé, *Georges Brassens,* Seghers (1963 coll. Poètes d'aujourd'hui; Poésie et Chansons no.2, 1988). Includes introductory essay by Lucien Rioux.
6. Jean-Michel Brial, *Brassens*, PAC, coll. Têtes d'affiche (1981).
7. Louis-Jean Calvet, *Georges Brassens*, Lieu Commun (1991), Payot, (1993).
8. Jacques Charpentreau, *Georges Brassens et la poésie quotidienne de la chanson*, Cerf, coll. Tout le monde en parle (1960).
9. André Comay, *32 chansons de Brassens expliquées à Marc et Denis*, Brenac, 1991.
10. René Fallet, *Brassens*, Denoël, 1967.
11. Paul Ghézi, *La Femme dans l'œuvre de Georges Brassens*, Talence, Presses Universitaires de Bordeaux (1991).
12. Linda Hantrais, *Le Vocabulaire de Georges Brassens* (vol. I), Klincksieck (1976).
13. André Larue, *Brassens ou la mauvaise herbe*, Fayard (1970).
14. Nicole Ligney et Cécile Abdesselam, *Brassens*, Bréa (1982).
15. Lucien Rioux, *Georges Brassens, le poète philosophe*, Seghers/Club des stars (1988).

16. Marc Robine et Thierry Séchan, *Georges Brassens, histoire d'une vie*, Fixot (1991), J'ai lu (1993).

16a. Loïc Rochard, *Brassens, orfèvre des mots*, Carnac, L. Rochard (1996).

17. André Sallée, *Brassens*, Solar (1991).

18. André Sève, *Brassens, toute une vie pour la chanson*, Centurion (1975).

19. André Tillieu, *Brassens auprès de son arbre*, Julliard (1983), Brussels, Lefrancq (1998).

20. Pol Vandromme, *Brassens, le petit père*, Brussels, Marc Laudelout (1983), La Table Ronde (1996).

21. Jacques Vassal, *Brassens ou la chanson d'abord*, Albin Michel (1991).

22. Fabrice Venturini, *Georges Brassens ou la parole distanciée*, Saint Genouph, Nizet, coll. Chanteurs-poètes (1996).

23. Marc Wilmet, *Georges Brassens libertaire*, Brussels, Les Eperonniers (1991).

24. *Brassens en bandes dessinées*, Vent d'Ouest (1989-90).

OTHER RELEVANT BOOKS ON LA CHANSON

25. Pierre Barbier et France Vernillat, *Histoire de la France par les chansons*, 8 vols, Gallimard (1956-61).

26. Pierre-Jean de Béranger, *Chansons* (1847), Edns. d'Aujourd'hui, 1983.

27. P. Brochon, *La Chanson sociale de Béranger à Brassens*, Edns. Ouvrières (1961).

28. Chantal Brunschwig, Louis-Jean Calvet, Jean-Claude Klein, *100 ans de la chanson française*, Seuil (1972).

29. Lucienne Cantaloube-Ferrieu, *Chanson et poésie des années 30 aux années 60*, Nizet (1981).

30. Luc Decaunes, *Les Très Riches Heures de la chanson française*, Seghers (1980).

31. Serge Dillaz, *Béranger*, Seghers (1971, coll. Poésie et Chansons no. 15).

32. —, *La Chanson française de contestation*, Seghers (1973).

33. Angèle Guller, *Le Neuvième Art: pour une connaissance de la chanson française contemporaine (de 1945 à nos jours)*, Brussels, Vokaer (1978).

34. André Halimi, *On connaît la chanson!*, La Table Ronde (1959).

35. Jean-Claude Klein, *Florilège de la chanson française*, Bordas, coll. Les compacts (1990).

36. Henry Poisot, *L'Age d'or de la chanson française*, Saint-Germain-des-Prés (1972).

37. René Ringeas et Gaston Coutant, *Gaston Coûté: l'enfant perdu de la révolte*, Saint-Ouen, Au Vieux Saint-Ouen (1966).

38. Lucien Rioux, *Vingt ans de chansons*, Arthaud (1966).

39. Marc Robine, *Anthologie de la chanson française*, Albin Michel (1994).

40. André Sallée et Philippe Chauveau, *Music-hall et café concert*, Bordas (1985).
41. Stéphane Strowski, *Béranger: textes choisis,* Plon (1913).
42. France Vernillat et Jacques Charpentreau, *La Chanson francaise*, Presses Universitaires de France, coll. Que sais-je? (1971).
43. Boris Vian, *En avant la zizique*, Le Livre Contemporain (1958), La Jeune Parque (1966).

CHAPTERS AND ARTICLES IN JOURNALS (in chronological order)

44. Louis Barjon, 'La chanson d'aujourd'hui', *Etudes*, vol. 294 (juillet-août-septembre 1957), pp.51-66.
45. Claude Marcheix, 'Aujourd'hui la chanson', *Tendances*, 37 (octobre 1965), pp.465-88.
46. Robert Poulet, 'Un genre avili', *Ecrits de Paris* (janvier 1968), pp.94-99.
47. Marc d'Eramo, 'La parole contestataire: Brassens et Dylan', *Cultures*, vol. II, 4 (1975), pp.56-105.
48. Colin Evans, 'Brassens, Thackray and the French folk tradition', *Recorded Sound* [London] (April-July 1977), pp.673-77.
49. Christopher Pinet, 'The Image of the French in the songs of Georges Brassens', *Contemporary French Civilization*, vol. VI, 1-2 (Fall-Winter 1981), pp.271-94.
50. — 'Astérix, Brassens, and Cabu: the ABCs of Popular Culture', in *Popular Traditions and Learned Culture in France*, ed. Marc Bertrand, Stanford French and Italian Studies, Stanford, Calif.: Anma Libri (1985), pp.275-86.

PRESS AND MAGAZINE ARTICLES (in chronological order)

51. Marcel Idzkowski, '2 révélations chez Patachou', *France-Soir*, 2373 (16.3.52), p.4.
52. Carmen Tessier, 'Deux soldats attaquent Georges Brassens chanteur antimilitariste', *France-Soir*, 2479 (19.7.52), p.1.
53. G. Joly, 'Aux Trois Baudets', *L'Aurore*, 2499 (25.9.52), p.2.
54. Henry Magnan, 'Aux Trois Baudets Georges Brassens troubadour gaillard', *Le Monde*, 2390 (2.10.52), p.12.
55. Paul Guth, 'Je chante pour les oreilles, pas pour les yeux', *Le Figaro Littéraire* (16.10.54), p.4.
56. R. Danger, 'Les bourgeois de la Baule m'ont épaté', *France-Soir*, 3422 (28.7.55), p.1.
57. Maurice Ciantar, 'Georges Brassens à l'Olympia', *Combat* 3507 (10.10.55), p.2.
58. Claude Sarraute, 'Georges Brassens et Christian Méry à Bobino', *Le Monde*, 3429 (1.02.56), p.8.

59. Claude Sarraute, 'Georges Brassens à l'Olympia', *Le Monde*, 3823 (9.5.57), p.12.

60. Serge, 'Georges Brassens à l'Olympia', *Les Nouvelles Littéraires*, 1551 (23.5.57), p.8.

61. Serge, 'La piste et la scène', *Les Nouvelles Littéraires*, 1571 (10.10.57), p.10.

62. Claude Sarraute, 'A l'Alhambra', *Le Monde*, 3960 (17.10.57), p.9.

63. 'T', 'Trois spectacles', *Le Canard enchaîné*, 2049 (27.1.60), p.6.

64. Claude Sarraute, 'Georges Brassens à l'Olympia', *Le Monde*, 5228 (8.11.61), p.13.

65. 'T', 'De Georges Brassens à Gaston Couté', *Le Canard enchaîné*, 2199 (12.12.62), p.5.

66. G. Bloch, 'Un poète populaire à Bobino', *L'Humanité* (16.9.63), p.2.

67. Michel Perrin, 'Brassens avec et sans musique', *Les Nouvelles Littéraires*, 1883 (3.10.63), p.10.

68. G. Bloch, 'A Bobino. Un faux pas de Brassens et une prouesse de Barbara', *L'Humanité*, 6278 (28.10.64), p.8.

69. André Wurmser, 'Georges Brassens défend ... l'indéfendable', *L'Humanité*, 6299 (24.11.64), p.8.

70. Claude Sarraute, 'Poésie et chanson', *Le Monde* (31.1.65), p.12.

71. Jean Serge, 'Brel et Brassens: quelques vérités sur nous-mêmes et les autres', *L'Express*, 759 (3.01.66), pp.30-32.

72. Danièle Heymann, 'Brassens repart en guerre', *L'Express*, 795 (12-18.9.66), pp.38-41.

73. Paul Carrière, 'Chanson au TNP Greco, Brassens', *Le Figaro*, 6270 (21.9.66), p.30.

74. Jean Monteaux, 'La France de Brassens, un authentique poète', *Arts et Loisirs* (janvier 1967), pp.12-14.

75. Alain Bosquet, 'Brassens? Pourquoi pas Fernandel?', *Combat* (10.6.67), p.20.

76. René Bourdier, 'Trois rendez-vous avec Brassens', *Les Lettres Françaises* (15-21.6.67), pp.25-26.

77. Jean-Pierre Chabrol, 'La Cour du roi Géo', *Le Figaro Littéraire* (25.6.67), pp.14-15.

78. Jean Patrick Maury, 'Brassens est-il un poète?', *Le Magazine littéraire* (juillet-août 1967), pp.28-30.

79. René Clair, 'Le rire de Brassens', *Les Nouvelles Littéraires*, 2104 (28.12.67), p.1.

80. Alain Bosquet, 'La page du poème inédit', *Le Quotidien de Paris* (1.12.81), p.24.

81. Christian Leblé [untitled], *Libération* (22.10.91), p.39.

SPECIAL ISSUES DEVOTED TO BRASSENS

82. *Paroles et Musique*, Brézolles, Edns de l'Araucaria, 41 (juin-août 1984). Major contributors: Jacques Vassal and Marc Robine.

83. *Vagabondages*, 59 (avril-juin 1985).
84. *Télérama* (Hors Série), 31 (octobre 1991). Articles cited:
Bernard Mérigaud, 'La Ballade du poète disparu', pp. 6–49.
Fabienne Pascaud, 'Misogynie à part, tu parles!', pp. 64–65.
85. *Chorus*, 17 (octobre-décembre 1996).

OTHER WORKS REFERRED TO

86. Jean Clouzet, *Brel*, Seghers, coll. Poètes d'aujourd'hui (1964).
87. Michèle Aquien, *La Versification*, Presses Universitaires de France, coll. Que sais-je? (1990).
88. André Vers, *C'était quand hier?*, Régine Deforges (1990).
89. Jean-Pierre Chabrol, *La Feloque des copains*, Les Presses du Languedoc (1987).
90. George Orwell, *Down and out in Paris and London* (1933), Harmondsworth: Penguin (1975).
91. George Melly, *Revolt into style*, Harmondsworth: Penguin (1970).
92. André Wyss, *Eloge du phrasé*, Presses Universitaires de France (1999).